The Random Book of...

ANDREW

Andrew Robinson

The Random Book of…

ANDREW

Well, I didn't know that!

All statistics, facts and figures are correct as of March 31st 2009.

© Andrew Robinson
Andrew Robinson has asserted his rights in accordance with the
Copyright, Designs and Patents Act 1988 to be identified
as the author of this work.

Published By:

Stripe Publishing Ltd
First Floor, 3 St. Georges Place, Brighton, BN1 4GA

Email: info@stripepublishing.co.uk
Web: www.stripepublishing.co.uk

First published 2009

A catalogue record for this book is available from the British Library.

10-digit ISBN: 1-907158-01-4
13-digit ISBN: 978-1-907158-01-8

Printed and bound by Gutenberg Press Ltd., Malta.

Editor: Dan Tester
Illustrations: Jonathan Pugh (www.pughcartoons.co.uk)
Typesetting: Andrew Searle
Cover: Andy Heath

INTRODUCTION

Andrew – that's a man's name. It means manly, and by goodness it sounds manly.

Try saying it yourself in two booming syllables: AN-DREW!

You could fell trees with a name like that, or command lions. No wonder it's so popular. It belonged to two Presidents of the United States and the second-richest man in the history of the world.

It's the name of Jesus' first Apostle, the home of golf, the fourth Bee Gee, the world's most famous musical theatre composer, the founder of Celtic Football Club and a rare species of beaked whale.

This book contains the untold – and randomised – heritage of Andrews, Andys, Drews and Roos the world over.

If you are one, or know one, you owe it to someone to buy this book.

Andrew Robinson – March 2009

WHAT'S IN A NAME?

Andrew comes from the Greek name Ανδρεας (Andreas), which was derived from ανηρ (aner), meaning 'man' or 'manly'.

The name first appears in text in the English translation of the Christian Bible's New Testament. Andrew was Jesus' first apostle. Considering the ensuing popularity of the name, it's ironic that we don't know what Andrew/Andreas was really called.

The New Testament, which many believe to have been originally written in Greek (others believe that it was translated to Greek from Hebrew), calls him Andreas.

But a humble Palestinian fisherman would not have had a Greek name.

Andrew derivations are very common throughout the Christian world, especially since the Middle Ages. In English, Andrew is most often shortened to Andy, Drew or Roo.

Looking for a derivative slant on the name Andrew? Let's ask our non-English speaking friends for help...

Aindreas: Scottish Gaelic
Anders: Danish, Finnish, Norwegian, Swedish
Andersine: Danish (female)
Andraž: Slovene
Andras: Hungarian
André: French

Andrea: Albanian, Italian (male); Croatian, Danish,
English, Finnish, German, Hungarian, Icelandic,
Norwegian, Spanish, Swedish (female)
André: Brazilian Portuguese
Andrej: Croatian, Slovene
Andreja: Croatian, Slovene (female)
Andreas: Austrian, Cyprian, Danish, Finnish, German,
Greek, Norwegian, Swedish
Andreia: Brazilian Portuguese (female)
Andrée: French (female)
Andrés: Spanish
Andrés: Icelandic
Andreus: Greek
Andrey: Russian
Andrew: English
Andrija: Croatian
Andrzej: Polish
Indri: Maltese

⊰―≺◆≻―⊱

Places and things

Andriyivskyy uzviz, literally translated from the Ukrainian
as **Andrew's Descent**, is a historic street in the Ukrainian
capital of Kiev.

Andrew Bay and **Andrew Lake** are the sunken remains
of a long-extinct volcano on Adak, a large island in the
central Aleutians.

There's a county called **Andrew** in Missouri, an **Andrew Bay** in Minnesota and another in Myanmar.

The world's largest model of a mallard duck is poised for take-off in **Andrew**, Alberta, Canada. It was built to commemorate the Whitford Lake wetland areas, a popular breeding ground for mallards. **Andrew Airport** is a mile north-west of the town.

Andrews Bald is a double-summit mountain standing 1804m above sea level in Swain County, North Carolina, in the Great Smoky Mountains. A bald is an upland grassed area.

Hurricane Andrew was the second most destructive hurricane in American history, causing 65 deaths. Andrew struck the Bahamas, southern Florida and Morgan City, Louisiana in August 1992, leaving a $26.5 billion trail of destruction. It was America's costliest natural disaster until Katrina in 2005.

The **Andrew File System** is a distributed networked file system developed by Carnegie Mellon University as part of the Andrew Project. Both Carnegie and Mellon were named Andrew (see the Wealthy section for more on these two magnates).

St. Andrews, on the east coast of Fife, houses Scotland's oldest university. Though its cathedral is now ruined, St. Andrews was, for centuries, the home of the Scottish Church. Now, it is better known for its golf, thanks to the Royal and Ancient Golf Club, which until recently set the rules for the global game. There's another golf course called St. Andrews in Kansas, USA.

Not surprisingly considering the spread of Christianity and the number and prominence of the Saints Andrew, there are countless places on Earth with the name.

Here are a couple of the more unspoiled examples:

The parish of **Saint Andrew, Barbados** is known for its green rolling hills and contains the country's highest natural elevation, Mount Hillaby. Barbados' most prestigious national award is **The Order of St Andrew**.

St. Andrew Bay, Florida, is a 69,000-acre estuary known for its biodiversity, seagrass beds, and its importance as a nursery for coastal fishery resources.

St. Andrew's Cathedral is a Gothic Revivalist edifice in the city of Sydney, Australia, and the seat of the Anglican Archbishop of Sydney.

St. Andrew-by-the-Wardrobe is a Christopher Wren-designed church which was founded in medieval times. It's on Queen Victoria Street near Blackfriars in the City of London. The wardrobe in the title belonged to Edward III, whose Royal Wardrobe was situated nearby. Both church and wardrobe were lost in the Great Fire of London, rebuilt by Wren in 1695, and bombed in World War II.

<hr />

ACTORS

As a character actor (where he is 'Andy', rather than his directorial moniker 'Andrew J.'), **Andrew J. Robinson** (b. 1942) was the punk who didn't feel lucky. He embodied one of the most killable characters in US cinema: the giggling, gibbering loon who hijacks a busload of children in 1971's *Dirty Harry*.

In his first acting part he bore the brunt of Clint Eastwood's most famous line, concerning the decapitation abilities of the Colt .44 Magnum, its six-shell capacity, the difficulty one might have in recalling how many shots had been fired and one's optimism on that score.

Robinson has since been a shoe-in for shady characters with anything from a thin slice to the whole iced cake of psychosis. While never quite making the A-list, Robinson has enjoyed a fine and full career, appearing in dozens of films, notably *Hellraiser*, almost 40 episodes of *Star Trek: Deep Space Nine* (as Elim Garak) and countless other US TV shows and stage plays.

Andy Garcia (b. 1956) is a real-life hero who saved the lives of a family after a boating accident off the coast of

Miami. Cuban-born Andrés Arturo García y Menéndez made his first big blip on the cinematic radar in Brian De Palma's *The Untouchables* in 1987.

In one of the film's key scenes, he earns a place on Eliot Ness's team by threatening to blow off Sean Connery's head. De Palma had seen Garcia in an episode of Hill Street Blues, and his subsequent casting led to a string of box-office hits.

He played Vincente Corleone in Francis Ford Coppola's *The Godfather III* – and was nominated for a Best Supporting Actor Oscar. Garcia has also played secondary roles in the string of 'Oceans' films alongside Clooney, Pitt et al. Garcia also wrote the soundtrack of *Ocean's 12* and is credited as composer on 2005's *The Lost City*, which he also directed.

Part of the US primetime televisual furniture for decades, and a man with an extraordinary quantity of teeth, **Andy Griffith** is best known for hundreds of appearances in two TV shows.

The Andy Griffith Show, in which he played Sheriff Andy Taylor, ran for 249 episodes between 1960 and 1968. Somewhat later in life he racked up 182 episodes of *Matlock* (in the title role of a cream-suited defence lawyer) between 1986 and 1995.

Griffith had first revealed serious acting credentials in the 1957 film *A Face in the Crowd*. His portrayal of a Machiavellian country boy who gains political power through a calculated use of televisual charisma was before its time, and its quality has been recognised only recently. He never won an Emmy throughout a long and illustrious career. Ironically, the second string to Griffith's bow has been more officially rewarding. His 1997 album of Christian hymns I Love to Say The Story won him a Grammy award. He is credited with 14 other recording albums.

Many fans thought **Andy Serkis** (b.1964) deserved an Oscar nomination for his portrayal of Gollum in the *Lord of the Rings* trilogy. Although the character was mainly envisioned in CGI (Computer-generated imagery), Serkis provided the human foundations on which the extraordinary animation was built.

He was originally hired only to provide the voice (inspired, he says, by a cat regurgitating a fur ball) but a two-week job turned into five years as his role in fleshing out the character grew. In his work for Peter Jackson, including *King Kong*, Middlesex-born Serkis has established himself as the world's best known 'performance capture' talent.

For this he wears a tight-fitting black suit covered in small bright blobs. His movements are filmed conventionally, and the blobs used as reference points for building realistic CGI movement. He'll reappear on-screen with a black beard and a fondness for the sauce as Captain Haddock in a series of *Tintin* films. Thundering typhoons!

Andy Clark, variously billed as Andrew J. Clark, A J. Clark and even Clarke, will be little known to today's

audiences, especially outside the United States. But
Andrews everywhere should revere him, because the
cinematic CV of this New York stage and vaudeville actor
is a lost treasure to the name. He began his film career in
the same year as (light bulb inventor and movie camera
pioneer) Thomas Edison and played 47 lead roles in 18
years.

In 1914 alone he appeared in *Andy Plays Hero*, *Andy Goes
on the Stage*, *Andy the Actor*, *Andy and the Hypnotist*, *Andy Plays
Cupid*, *Andy Goes A-Pirating*, *Andy Has a Toothache*, *Andy Learns
to Swim*, *Getting Andy's Goat*, *Andy and the Redskins*, *Andy Falls
in Love*, *The Adventures of Andy Clark* (as himself) and seven
other 'Andy' films. He single-handedly put the name Andy
on the cinematic map in a film career that flew through
the Twenties but ended abruptly with the onset of the
Depression in 1930. Andy Clark died in 1960.

Actor and comedian **Andy Dick** (b. 1965) is best known
in the UK for his sitcom work – as Matthew Brock on
NewsRadio in the Nineties and Owen Kronsky in *Less Than
Perfect* from 2002. Dick began his TV career as a regular
cast member on *The Ben Stiller Show* in the early 1990s and
has appeared on countless TV shows.

In character or as himself, he is a regular voice artist,
writer, director, producer and generator of outraged
headlines in the press. He has been forcibly dragged from
the stage after offending other guests on chat shows, and
been arrested for indecent exposure and drug possession.

His public indecency and drunkenness tend to have gone hand-in-hand, but his potential to entertain has made him a regular guest on big US talk shows such as *Late Show with David Letterman* and *Jimmy Kimmel Live*. Dick's CV is littered with guest appearances, and between 2001 and 2003 he even had his very own *The Andy Dick Show* for three seasons. Career highlights include voicing characters for *The Simpsons* and *Happily N'Ever After*, while filling character roles in two or three feature films and TV series per year.

Balamory fans will know Scottish actor **Andrew Agnew** (b. 1976) as PC Plum. Since the Bafta-winning pre-schoolers' favourite Agnew has been directing a new programme called *Me Too*, and doing a bit of panto.

The man behind the leather face in both recent Texas Chainsaw Massacre movies – the 2003 remake and the 2006 prequel – was reportedly discovered by a talent-spotter while visiting Hollywood. **Andrew Bryniarski** (b. 1969) landed a role in Bruce Willis's expensive 1991 folly *Hudson Hawk* before landing a series of large, very muscular roles in such films as *Any Given Sunday* and *Pearl Harbor*.

Actor and Labour MP **Andrew Faulds** first came to public attention as a radio performer before joining the Royal Shakespeare Company in 1948. He and his wife, the marvellously named Bunty Whitfield, were friends of the politically active American singer-actor Paul Robeson

(famous in the UK for his recording of 'Ol' Man River'),
and hosted Robeson when he came to play Othello with
the RSC at Stratford.

Faulds gained the Smethwick seat for Labour in the 1964
General Election and held it until his retirement in 1997.
For the first two decades of his political career, in the era
of Enoch Powell, Faulds continued his acting career. He
was a favourite of loopy/visionary director Ken Russell,
appearing in *The Devils* (1971), *The Music Lovers* (1971),
Mahler (1974) and *Lisztomania* (1975). Glenda Jackson, who
also became a Labour MP, shared the screen with him in
The Music Lovers.

A former stand-up comedian and the brother of Frances de
la Tour (the object of Rigsby's ardour in *Rising Damp*), **Andy
de la Tour** is also an actor. He was in *Notting Hill*, Polanski's
Oliver Twist and *Plenty*, and has written for various British TV
series including *Boon*, *Peak Practice* and *Kavanagh QC*.

Although he's remembered primarily as the cowering
Spanish waiter Manuel in all 12 episodes of Fawlty Towers,
Andrew Sachs has a full and illustrious CV stretching in
both directions from this mid-1970s milestone. Sachs was
born Andreas Siegfried Sachs in Berlin in 1930, and fled
with his parents to Britain just before Kristallnacht.

From the late 1950s to the 1970s, Sachs appeared in many
staple TV series of the time, including *The Saint*, *ITV
Playhouse*, *Fraud Squad*, *Randall & Hopkirk (Deceased)*, *Callum*

and *Are You Being Served?* He also had a bit part in movie *The Revenge of the Pink Panther* (as Hercule Poirot).

As Manuel, Sachs twice received semi-serious injuries. He was almost concussed by a large frying pan wielded by John Cleese, and was once scarred by acid applied to his clothing to replicate fire. He released four single EPs as Manuel, including a version of Shaddap You Face. Post-Fawlty, Sachs' skilled but unassuming presence continued to win him minor parts in four or five TV productions per year, but it is in voice work that he has really made his mark.

His most recent 'appearance', in 2008, precipitated the suspension of Jonathan Ross and the resignation of Russell Brand. BBC Radio 2 broadcast a recording of the pair leaving a series of 'rather crude' (Sachs' words) messages on his answerphone.

The Amphion-class Royal Navy submarine **HMS Andrew** played the role of the fictional nuclear-powered USS Sawfish in the 1959 movie *On the Beach*. The WWII sub also had the distinction of having been the first to cross the Atlantic underwater.

Drew Barrymore's real first name is Andrew.

ANIMALISTIC ANDREWS

You won't have seen one of these before; I doubt if even
David Attenborough has made its acquaintance. He'd
remember if he had, because *Mesoplodon bowdoini* – or
Andrew's Beaked Whale – is among the rarest and most
peculiar beings to bear the name Andrew. In most respects,
it's a standard small whale/porpoise shape.

But the males have a pair of exposed bottom teeth that
rise up alongside the nose, like boars' tusks. In fact, many
male members of the Beaked Whale family have such
gnashers. The cetaceans grow up to about five metres in
length and are mainly found in the Southern Hemisphere
near the Antipodes. They have rarely been seen alive in the
wild: most of our knowledge comes from the few that have
washed up on the shores of New Zealand and Australia.

Meanwhile, *Bunomys Andrewsi* – **Andrew's Hill Rat** – is
another rare non-human Andrew. It only exists in Indonesia
and is on the IUCN endangered species Red List.

ANDREW ARCHITECTS

Although his own villas, palaces and churches are found in
only a small area of Italy, around Venice and Vincenza, the
influence of **Andrea Palladio** encompassed the world.

It was still informing architecture hundreds of years after
his death in 1580. 'Palladian' can be used to describe an

enormous number of significant buildings. In Britain, Inigo Jones, Christopher Wren and Lord Burlington all built mansions and churches in his style. Chiswick House, Blenheim Palace, Houghton Hall and many other British colonial, American, French and, of course, Italian buildings are Palladian in style.

Palladio designed along classical Roman lines, with a great sense of aesthetic proportion and a central edifice that conveyed the importance of the building and especially its owner or contents.Even relatively humble British Victorian homes, with their brick and stucco walls, reveal his influence.

Andrew Willatsen was a German-born architect, mainly working in the first few decades of the 20th century in Seattle and north-west USA. An apprentice of Frank Lloyd Wright, he left the studio after a few years to join a studio in Seattle and subsequently formed a long-lasting creative partnership with former Lloyd Wright colleague Barry Byrne. Both are credited with spreading the influence of Frank Lloyd Wright and the Prairie Style across north-west America.

ANDREW ARTISTS

Andrew Bell (1726-1809) was a well known Edinburgh engraver, responsible for the majority of the engravings for the *Britannica*, which he later came to own outright.

King George III took offence at his highly descriptive images of a foetus in the womb and the female pelvic region, and ordered the pages ripped from every copy. Bell's appearance was almost as noticeable as his work. Although only four-and-a-half feet tall, he rode an enormous horse and had the habit of enlarging his already impressive nose with papiermaché.

Andrew Warhola (b. 1928) – perhaps the best known artist (as **Andy Warhol**) of the late 20th century – bridged the gap between commercial and fine art, and spearheaded the Pop Art movement. He was a highly successful commercial illustrator for magazines and advertising, and latterly album covers, in the 1950s.

In the 1960s, Warhol painted his famous mass-produced products – Campbell's Tomato Soup cans, Brillo boxes etc. – and silk-screen prints of celebrities such as Marilyn Monroe and Elizabeth Taylor. Some didn't think the results were art, and galleries initially refused to exhibit his work.

But within a few years Warhol had become the most talked-about and commercially successful artist of his era. He was certainly one of the richest in his own lifetime, heading up various studios, most famously The Factory.

He directed and/or produced countless art films, mainly with sexual titles (*Blow Job* etc.). Warhol coined the prescient "15 minutes of fame" well before today's plethora of short-term celebrities.

He was never the healthiest-looking specimen. Sickly as a child, he suffered from St Vitus' Dance, a nervous-system disease that causes skin blotching. He became something of a hypochondriac with a fear of hospitals. He almost died in 1968 when he and art critic Mario Amaya were shot by radical feminist Valerie Solanas in Warhol's studio. It took direct heart massage to save his life. He eventually did die from an unexpected heart attack while recovering from a gall bladder operation in 1987.

Artist **Andrew Vicari** – reported to be the wealthiest artist in the world with a personal fortune of £92m – took some credit for Stoke City FC's promotion to the First Division in 2002.

The Welshman, who owes much of his wealth to painting portraits of the Saudi Royal Family, had been called in on the advice of a feng shui expert to paint a mural in the 'room of doom', the south end changing room.

The idea was to banish bad spirits believed to have caused a string of defeats for teams using the south changing room in major play-offs and finals. Vicari took about an hour to paint the mural incorporating the sun, a phoenix and a horse on the changing room wall.

Andrew Dasburg, who died in 1979, was one of America's leading Modernist painters. Born in Paris, he was raised in New York's Hell's Kitchen before an art teacher spotted his talent and negotiated a scholarship for him.

An acquaintance of Matisse, whom he watched paint in
about 1909, he was mainly inspired by Cezanne. Much
of his work, which influenced American art throughout
the 20th century, was mildly cubist – featuring disjointed
subjects and perspectives – in the Cezanne manner.

To give you a quick flavour of eccentric British performance
artist, sculptor and fashionista **Andrew Logan** (b. 1945),
here's the judging panel from his latest (2004) Alternative
Miss World competition: Pete Doherty (pop artist), Peter
Blake (Turner Prize winner), Greyson Perry, Brian Eno,
Zandra Rhodes (Bad Girls), Amanda Barrie, Boy George
and Sian Phillips.

The Alternative Miss World has been running, on and
off, since 1972. By all accounts, the events are *outrageous*.
Flamboyant, fun-loving Logan has cut a camp figure on the
British art scene since the early 1970s. He was a friend of
Derek Jarman, whose early films were shot around Logan's
Butler's Wharf studios.

The building was also the setting for Vivienne Westwood
and Malcolm McLaren's famous 1976 Valentine's Ball, and
an early venue for the Sex Pistols. Logan works with found
materials, creating enormous winged horses or thrones in
the form of flowers.

André Derain (b. 1880) was a co-founder of Fauvism
with his friend Henri Matisse. They worked together
in 1905 and produced a series of paintings with vivid,

unnatural colours, which led a critic to call them les Fauves, or wild beasts.

In 1906 Derain was sent by a dealer to London, to compose a series of paintings. His bold vibrant renditions of the Thames and Tower Bridge are still his best and most popular works.

As the NASA satellite pictures that make up Google Earth get clearer, so the service has become an online art gallery for those whose works are large enough to be seen from space. Australian sculptor **Andrew Rogers'** work is among those worth peering down at.

Though Rogers gained his reputation through more conventionally sized bronze pieces, his 'geoglyphs' are earning plenty of attention. He has installed huge stone sculptures, intended to be viewed from above, in many of the world's most remote, beautiful or historic places: the Gobi desert, Israel's Arava desert plus locations in Chile, Bolivia and Australia, to name a few. His website www. andrewrogers.org gives map co-ordinates you can use for locating them on Google Earth.

American artist **Andrew Wyeth** (1917-2009) is best known for his 1948 painting *Christina's World*. It depicts Christina Olson, who suffered a muscle-wasting disease in her lower body, resolutely dragging herself across a field towards her farmhouse home. Although Wyeth was a friend of the Olsons, his wife was supposedly the model for the painting.

He also gained notoriety after unveiling 247 previously unknown paintings of his neighbour, Helga. As an ongoing study of a single person's physiognomy, the series is unique in the art world. Although the series is now owned by a Japanese collector, Wyeth added one final painting – *Gone* – in 2002.

Andrew Wyeth died peacefully in his sleep at his home in Pennsylvania, after a brief illness, on January 16th, 2009.

The son of a Maths professor, Cheshire-born **Andy Goldsworthy** (b. 1956) spent some time as a farm labourer before studying art. He has spent 30-odd years creating temporary outdoor works from found natural objects such as leaves, petals, icicles, sticks and pebbles; and permanent installations from stone.

He likens the repetitive processes of farm labour to the creation of his artworks, many of which draw on the patterns and repetitions found in nature. He's the author and photographer of 18 books depicting his work.

Glaswegian sculptor **Andy Scott** will be well known to anyone commuting along the M8 past his four-metre-high *Heavy Horse*, at Glasgow Business Park. Scott is a figurative sculptor and mainly uses bronze, steel and fibreglass.

Among his most interesting new projects is *The Kelpies*, two enormous horse heads which are planned as part of the Helix boat-lift system on the Forth and Clyde Canal near

Falkirk. Kelpies in this instance are not Australian dogs, but mythical Celtic water horses said to haunt the natural waterways of Ireland and Scotland.

Andy Capp was a regular and very popular cartoon in northern editions of *The Daily Mirror* from 1957. The flat cap-wearing anti-hero husband of long-suffering Flo, Andy and his wife were based on the parents of their creator, Reginald Smythe.

Andy Capp is now syndicated in 50 countries and 700 publications. Andy is also known as André Chapeau (France), Tuffa Viktor (Sweden), Kasket Karl (Denmark) and Willi Wacker (Germany). He has spawned a TV series by Keith Waterhouse (starring James Bolam in the title role), a West End musical and a variety of spicy corn chip.

If you ever visit Stavanger Cathedral in Norway, take a good look at the pulpit. It's the work of Scottish craftsman and painter **Andrew Lawrenceson Smith**. Finished in 1658, it's regarded as a highly significant work of baroque Norwegian art.

ASTRONAUTS

Lt Col. **Andrew M. Allen** flew three NASA missions aboard the space shuttles *Atlantis* and *Columbia* between 1992 and 1996. He has orbited Earth 602 times, covering 15.6 million miles. A graduate of the 'Top Gun' Naval Fighter Weapons School, Allen has been awarded three honorary doctorates and countless distinguished service awards. He retired in 1997.

From the other side of the planet, and with at least 3,000 Earth orbits under his belt, is Australian aerospace engineer and NASA astronaut **Andy Thomas PhD**. A former Lockheed aerodynamics engineer, Thomas joined NASA in 1993.

After additional training in Russia, Thomas spent 130 days on board the Mir Space Station (which was decommissioned in 2001). He flew with space shuttles *Endeavour* and also *Discovery* on its 2005 'Return to Flight' mission (the first shuttle flight since the 2003 *Columbia* disaster). He is married to another NASA astronaut, Shannon Walker.

———◆◆◆———

ASTRONOMERS

André Patry was a 20th century French astronomer who worked at the Observatoire de Nice from the age of 17. He died in his late 50s but not before discovering nine asteroids.

Asteroid 1601 Patry is named after him. His contemporary, **André-Louis Danjon**, devised a way to measure 'Earthshine' (the extent to which the Earth illuminates the moon). Danjon also designed the highly accurate Danjon astrolabe and was Director of the Paris Observatory from 1945 to 1963.

Asteroid 27130 Dipaola is named after **Andrea Di Paola**, a contemporary Italian astronomer at the Osservatorio Astronomico di Roma.

Andreas Cellarius, who produced the famous star atlas Harmonia Macrocosmica in 1660, has the minor planet 12618 Cellarius named in his honour.

Greek-born NASA astrophysicist **Dr. Andy Michalitsianos** worked for many years at the Goddard Space Flight Centre, and was heavily involved with the Hubble Space Telescope project.

He won several awards for his contribution to the International Ultraviolet Explorer and eventually became Chief of the Laboratory for Astronomy and Solar Physics, making famous strides in his research on symbiotic stars. He died of a brain tumour in 1997; the Andreas Gerasimos Michalitsianos robotic telescope is named after him.

An 1883 photograph of the Orion Nebula was perhaps the crowning achievement of **Andrew Ainslie Common**, the Newcastle-upon-Tyne astronomer-photographer. As well as observing the moons of Mars and Saturn in the 19th century, he also built telescopes. He was President of the Royal Astronomical Society from 1895 to 1896.

Comet expert **Andrew Claude de la Cherois Crommelin** was an Irish astronomer who proved that three comets – Forbes, Coggia-Winnecke and Pons – were in fact one and the same. Though this initially meant it became Comet Pons-Coggia-Winnecke-Forbes, the astral body is now simply named 27/P Crommelin.

His name also went to the Moon's Crommelin crater, Mars's Crommelin crater and the asteroid 1899 Crommelin. He died in 1939.

Thanks to **Andrew Gemant**'s endowment to the American Institute of Physics, the Andrew W. Gemant Award annually recognises significant contributions to the cultural, artistic or humanistic dimension of physics.

The 2007 award went to **Andrew Fraknoi** of Foothill College in Los Altos, California, for more than 30 years work as a teacher, public lecturer, co-author/editor of a syndicated astronomy newspaper column, host/producer of a weekly radio show and numerous guest appearances on national radio and TV.

Fraknoi is the lead author of *Voyages through the Universe*, an astronomy college textbook, and also wrote *Wonderful World of Space*, published by Disney.

Irish astronomer **Andrew Graham** developed the square-bar micrometer, which increased the efficiency of celestial object positioning. He discovered the asteroid 9 Metis in 1848 and was an author of the *Markree Catalogue*, a recording of 60,000 stars.

<hr/>

ANDREWS IN THE CINEMA

An Italian spoof of the Superman franchise, **SuperAndy**, Il fratello brutto di Superman (*SuperAndy, The Ugly Brother of Superman*) had Andy Luotto in the title role.

The plot? SuperAndy arrives in Italy after the destruction of Krypton, his home planet.

When Andrew Came Home or **Taming Andrew** (UK title) was a 2000 television film directed by Artie Mandelberg.

Originally a special-effects supervisor for Batman and James Bond films, multi-talented **Andrew Adamson** has two major franchises to his name: Shrek and Narnia.

He directed, wrote songs and provided voices for *Shrek* and *Shrek 2*, and also produced *Shrek The Third*. He's written and directed the first two Narnias – *The Lion, the Witch and the Wardrobe* and *Prince Caspian* – and produced the third, *The Voyage of the Dawn Treader*.

The original screenplay for Mel Brooks's comedy Western *Blazing Saddles* is perhaps his best known early work, but **Andrew Bergman** has been behind several other cult classics.

He wrote or co-wrote the films *The In-Laws*, *Fletch* and *Soapdish*, wrote and directed *The Freshman*, *Honeymoon in Vegas* and *It Could Happen To You*, and wrote and produced *Striptease*.

Bergman is also a novelist: *The Big Kiss-Off of 1944*, *Hollywood and LeVine*, *Tender Is LeVine* and *Sleepless Nights* bear his name. He also penned the Broadway comedy, *Social Security*. In 2007, Bergman received the Writers Guild of America's Ian McLellan Hunter Award for Lifetime Achievement in Writing.

Andrew Birkin (b. 1945) is a BAFTA winning screenwriter, actor and director. He is the brother of actress Jane Birkin, uncle of actress Charlotte Gainsbourg, father of actor David, the late poet and musician Anno and the young actor Ned.

He directed *Charlotte and Ned in the Cement Garden*, while his other cinematic writing credits include *Omen III*, *The Name of the Rose, Perfume, Slade in Flame, Sredni Vashtar, Burning Secret* and *The Lost Boys*. He also authored *J. M. Barrie* and *Lost Boys*.

Andrew Jones (b. 1983) is a young rising writer/ director/producer and film-maker. His first script, *Stray Dogs*, earned him enough US dollars to set up Steel and Glass Films in Swansea; then he worked as a painter-decorator to raise funds for *Teenage Wasteland*. Shot on a borrowed video camera using many non-actors, the film won Best Feature Under 75 Minutes at the 2006 Swansea Bay Film Festival.

His next project, *The Feral Generation*, an urban drama about two young lovers living rough and coping with heroin addiction, raised half a million pounds of backing and won Best UK Feature Film at the 2007 Swansea Life Film Festival.

Next in the pipeline is *The Beautiful Outsiders*, a road movie, and a £2.5million remake of *The Driller Killer*.

Andrew Lesnie's career high has so far been the 2002 Oscar for Best Cinematography for his work on *The Lord of the Rings: The Fellowship of the Ring*. His CV reads like a list of visually stunning movies. He was director of photography for the entire *Lord of the Rings* trilogy, *King Kong*, *I Am Legend*, both *Babe* movies and at least 20 others.

He also edited *The Sixth Sense*, *The Shipping News*, *Chocolat* and *What's Eating Gilbert Grape?* As you might expect, his list of awards is as long as your leg.

He was also chief cinematographer for *The Lovely Bones*.

Pixar's technical brilliance is rightly celebrated, but it was the stories of films like *WALL-E*, *Finding Nemo*, *Monsters, Inc.*, *Toy Story* and *A Bug's Life* that made them great. **Andrew Stanton** (b. 1965) wrote the story and screenplay for both *Toy Story* movies and *Finding Nemo*, and the screenplay for *WALL-E* and *Monsters, Inc.* He's also behind the screenplay for *John Carter of Mars*, and was the voice of Fred in *Cars*.

Hang on through the credits of some recent hits, like *Indiana Jones and the Crystal Skull*, *Kung Fu Panda*, *The Simpsons Movie*, *Blood Diamond*, *Die Hard 4.0* and *Mission Impossible III* and **Andy Nelson's** name will scroll past under 'Sound Re-recording Mixer'.

What does he do?

He mixes re-recorded sound, and he's done it on 137 films.

In 1999, perhaps the hottest Andrew in the movies was **Andy Wachowski** (b. 1967), one of the Wachowski Brothers, the former comic book artists who made *The Matrix* trilogy.

Former TV commercial director **Andrew Niccol** broke into Hollywood with scripts that became the films *Gattaca* and *The Truman Show*.

Imagine waking up each morning next to Galadriel, or alternatively Queen Elizabeth I. Sounds potentially confusing, but it's the happy fate of playwright, producer, director and 'Mr. Cate Blanchett' **Andrew Upton** (b. 1966).

He wrote, produced and directed *Bangers* in 1999, which starred Ms. Blanchett, and was co-writer of 2007 Aussie horror flick *Gone*. Upton wrote adaptations of *Hedda Gabler*, *The Cherry Orchard*, *Cyrano de Bergerac* and *Don Juan* for the Sydney Theatre Company (of which he and Blanchett are joint artistic directors), and Maxim Gorky's *The Philistines* for London's Royal National Theatre.

In 2007 his play *Riflemind* opened in Sydney, starring Hugo Weaving, and in 2008 he wrote the libretto for the opera *Through The Looking Glass* (by Alan Johns).

Andrew Bujalski is the American independent film writer-director-actor behind *Funny Ha Ha* (2005) and *Mutual Appreciation* (2006). With scripts that appear improvised, he has often been compared with British director Mike Leigh.

THE ANDREW COMPANY

Andrew is a company that makes wireless communications systems. It recently won a commission to install wireless on the new high-speed Beijing-Tianjin railway line.

Matt Melester, vice president and general manager, said: "Andrew is proud to help in the rapid development of China's rail transportation."

———◆———

ERRANT ANDREWS

Australian **Andrew Chan** (b. 1984) was sentenced to death by an Indonesian court after being found guilty of conspiring to smuggle heroin (into Australia) with eight accomplices in 2005. Several of the 'mules' caught with heroin strapped to their bodies claimed Chan had threatened them and their families.

Now, after three years on death row, all but three of the 'Bali Nine' have had their death sentences repealed. Chan and two accomplices still face execution, despite calls from John Howard that their lives be spared.

In 2002, after being indicted on 78 counts of money-laundering, fraud and conspiracy while chief financial officer of Enron Corp., **Andrew Fastow** (b. 1961) was sentenced to six years in prison. Fastow had been a major player in the multi-layered concealment of the company's losses, but reduced his sentence by helping the authorities secure further convictions of Enron personnel.

The heir to the Max Factor fortune, **Andrew Luster** (b. 1963) is currently serving his sixth year of a 124-year sentence. He was convicted by a jury on 86 counts of rape and other sexual offences, mostly using date-rape drug GHB. Luster went on the run and the trial was conducted in his absence while he continued to live off his $3.1 million trust fund.

He was captured by Duane 'Dog' Chapman's team of bounty hunters (filmed for his *Dog the Bounty Hunter* TV show) in Mexico. Chapman, though, was not entitled to any of the £1 million bounty, and was arrested himself for deprivation of liberty because bounty-hunting is not legal in Mexico.

According to Leeds City Council, **Andrew Kellett** is Britain's Dumbest Criminal. He posted more than 80 clips of his antisocial antics on YouTube, and was rewarded with an interim Asbo in May 2008, aged 23. He boasted that he'd had 285,000 hits, but clearly hadn't anticipated that some viewers might have been police.

A couple of prominent American mobster bosses for you.

New Yorker **Andrew Russo** is believed to be the acting boss of the Colombo crime family. He was released from prison in 2006 after a conviction for racketeering and is thought to have returned to the top job.

Andrew Thomas DelGiorno, known as Tommy Del, is a former captain in the Philadelphia crime family, associate of crime boss Nicky Scarfo and FBI informant. He concealed his Polish heritage to gain acceptance into the mob.

<hr>

MURDERING ANDREWS

Andrew Kehoe (b. 1872) killed 45 and injured 58 people, most of them young children, in the worst atrocity ever to take place at a United States school.

Kehoe blamed a new tax levied to help fund the construction of school buildings for his financial problems. In fact, his own chronic mismanagement was to blame. Still, Kehoe spent several months secreting large quantities of explosives around the Bath Consolidated School, of which he was a board member.

On receiving a notice of intent to repossess his farm, Kehoe set his plans in motion. On May 18th, 1927 – after first taking care to kill his wife and set fire to his farm buildings – he detonated the first bomb under the north wing of the school.

He then drove his shrapnel-loaded vehicle up to a group of school officials and children, and detonated his second bomb. This killed Kehoe and several bystanders, including the school superintendent. A large quantity of undetonated explosives was subsequently discovered in the basement of the school's south wing.

At age 11, **Andrew Golden** was one of the two perpetrators (with his cousin Mitchell Johnson) of the March 1998 Jonesboro school massacre. After setting off a fire alarm, Golden turned his rifle on fellow pupils, killing two girls and injuring another before being disarmed. Johnson killed two girls and a teacher. Golden was released from prison in 2008, aged 21, and is living under an alias in Arkansas.

When **Brenda Andrew**'s husband, Rob, was gunned down outside their house, she blamed masked assailants. But the mother of two planned the murder with fellow Sunday school teacher and lover James Pavatt.

They lost out on the $800,000 in life insurance.

Although his most famous victim was Gianni Versace, the clothing magnate was one of six people 27-year-old **Andrew Phillip Cunanan** slayed during a three-month road trip in 1997. The last was himself.

Andrew Lee Jones is the only American Andrew to have been executed for murder in modern times, and the last to be dispatched by the Louisiana State electric chair. He beat, raped and strangled 11-year-old Tumekica Jackson, the daughter of his estranged lover.

The Rostov Ripper, The Butcher of Rostov, The Red Ripper – call him what you will – killed at least 52 women and children in the former Soviet Union, mostly in the 1980s. His real name was **Andrei Romanovich Chikatilo**.

Royal Scots corporal **Andrew Walker** was jailed for life after a conviction for killing three of his colleagues during a payroll robbery in 1985. Unfortunate teenager Andrew Lowden, who shared a cell with Walker while on remand, claimed Walker threatened to kill Lowden's father and girlfriend if he did not deliver a letter placing the blame on the Provisional IRA.

The letter was intercepted and Andrew Lowden then played a crucial role in Walker's conviction.

In 1826 lawyers **Andrew Knapp** and William Baldwin published a collection of 'improving' tales that recounted the lives and crimes of notorious ne'er-do-wells from the preceding two centuries.

Called *The Newgate Calendar*, the stories were originally the monthly bulletin of the keeper of London's Newgate prison. By the mid-19th century, *The Newgate Calendar* was among the most popular books in Britain. One entry describes the exploits of **Andrew Rutherford**, and the ripe, richly partisan language deserves some unedited repetition.

"Andrew Rutherford was accused of having conceived deadly malice against James Douglass; that having dined together in a farmer's house on the 9th of July preceding, in company with several gentlemen, he, urged by this malevolent passion, on their way home from dinner, within half-a-mile of the town of Jedburgh, did murder Douglass, by giving him a mortal wound with a small sword through the arm, and through the body under the right pap, of which wounds he died within four hours; that he immediately fled to England, and would have embarked at South Shields, for Holland, had he not been apprehended."

Rutherford was beheaded on 25th November that year.

⇒•⇐

NOT GUILTY ANDREWS

Australian **Andrew Mallard** received a life sentence for murdering Pamela Lawrence in 1995 but was released 11 years later when it emerged that his conviction rested on suspiciously thin evidence and an incomplete disclosure of crucial information.

Even though the charges against Mallard were dropped on his release, he was still named as the prime suspect – until a 2006 police review of the investigation led to convicted murderer Simon Rochford being charged for the crime instead.

Rochford killed himself in his cell shortly after his police interview.

The case of **Andrew Evans** is perhaps the most bizarre in the modern history of miscarried British justice. Evans confessed to police after dreaming of the face of 14-year-old murder victim Judith Roberts.

He did not recall the crime but asked police to see a picture of the girl, and said: "I wonder if I've done it." More than 25 years passed before the Court of Appeal set him free after the conviction was declared unsafe. The Court of Appeal was told that Evans had suffered 'false memory' because of anxiety.

It was the damaging comments about the defendant made by jurors outside the courtroom that initially brought the case of **Andrew Adams** back to court 14 years after his conviction for murder. Adams was jailed in 1993 for the murder of science teacher Jack Royal, but the appeal court found that his defence had been inadequately prepared, and had not presented evidence that would have cleared Adams.

Andrew didn't kill Andrew, says Andrew

Following the 2007 acquittal of **Andrew Adams** (above), his story becomes an unlikely concatenation of Andrews. Adams' fellow inmate at Frankland Prison in Durham, **Andrew Davies**, is also serving a life sentence for murder. And, like Adams, he claims to be a victim of a miscarriage of justice. Davies was convicted of shooting **Andrew Landsdown** in North Tyneside, in 2000.

ANDREW THE ENGINEER

Anyone who's studied the subject, even if no deeper than Top Trumps level, will know there have been many Russian aircraft beginning with 'Tu'.

Andrei Nikolayevich Tupolev, a close friend of Nikita Khrushchev (Soviet president 1958-64), designed and project-managed dozens of aircraft through the middle part of the 20th century. Most notable were the Tu-95, a turboprop strategic bomber from the late 1950s, and the Tu-104 jet airliner – for some time the only jet passenger craft in continual service.

This airliner spawned a series of successors, culminating in the world's first supersonic airliner, the Tu-144. This craft, which just pre-dated the similar-looking Concorde in 1968, was designed by his son, Alexei. Andrei Tupolev died in 1972.

Scot **Andrew Barclay**, whose conglomeration of family companies eventually became Andrew Barclay Sons & Co., built locomotives throughout the 19th century. He churned out simple, tough machines employing steam, and later diesel, propulsion from his Kilmarnock plant.

Barclay specialised in fireless locomotives, powered by an onboard steam reservoir charged by an external boiler. These were used in areas where naked flame was unsafe or cleanliness paramount, such as mines or food factories. The company's name lives on, after a number of ownership changes, in the Brush-Barclay locomotive maintenance firm.

"Only the paranoid survive." Such was the motto of the intensely competitive man behind Intel. Charting the company's rise from chip maker to processor giant was Hungarian-American chemical engineer **Andrew Grove** (b. 1936).
The third member of the company, Grove became its president in 1979, its CEO in 1987 and its Chairman and CEO in 1997. He managed a 45-fold increase in Intel's market share, making it temporarily the world's most highly valued company. He resigned from the board in 2004 but

remains a senior advisor. Grove was named *Time* magazine's Man of the Year in 1997.

⇒◆⇐

FICTIONAL ANDREWS

Andy Pandy made a TV comeback in 2002 after disappearing for more than 30 years. He was first seen in 1950 and entertained very young children for 20 years. *Andy Pandy* was created by Freda Lingstrom, head of BBC children's television between 1951 and 1956, and Maria Bird.

It was part of the *Watch with Mother* slot. The stories were narrated by Vera McKechnie and the puppets made by a craftsman living in the same town – Westerham, in Kent – as Lingstrom and Bird. The pair formed Westerham Arts Films, which sold the episodes to the BBC. On his 2002 comeback, Andy was still accompanied by old friends Looby Loo and Teddy, but he wore trainers instead of clogs and lost the strings in his new stop-motion world.

Pre-dating Andy Pandy in the US was **Andy Panda**, a cartoon panda with his own series between 1939 and 1949. Andy was voiced by Bernice Hansen, then Sara Berner and finally Walter Tetley. His main claim to fame is that a 1940 episode called Knock Knock introduced a new character called Woody Woodpecker. Andy Panda later reappeared as a comic book and made a brief cameo in *Who Framed Roger Rabbit*.

One of Britain's favourite comedy sketches, according to a '100 Best…' programme involves **Lou and Andy** from *Little Britain*. Matt Lucas's Andy runs to a high-diving board, jumps off the top, swims back across the pool and arrives in his wheelchair while Lou's back is turned. What a kerfuffle.

Sir Andrew Aguecheek is the 'dear little puppet' of Sir Toby Belch in Shakespeare's *Twelfth Night*. He is one of Shakespeare's most demonstrably dim-witted, comic characters.

In C. S. Lewis's *The Magician's Nephew* – the book he later wrote as a prequel to *The Lion, The Witch and The Wardrobe* – the children Digory and Polly are transported to The Wood Between The Worlds by yellow rings made by Digory's **Uncle Andrew**. Although he's the magician in the title, Andrew Ketterley's magical powers are limited. He begins the story as a powerful and intimidating figure but is soon dwarfed by the powers of Queen Jadis and Aslan.

Raggedy Ann, a rag doll children's character who appeared in books just after the First World War, was eventually joined by her brother, **Raggedy Andy**.
Ten-year-old Andrew Dubble is the hero of the **Andrew Lost** series of children's books by J. C. Greenburg. There are 18 books in the series, produced between 2002 and 2008. Andrew is an inventor, but not a very good one. The stories mainly concern his attempts to set right the problems caused by his engineering.

The first of many books by 1920s/30s US children's writer Edward Edson Lee, writing under the pseudonym Leo Edwards, was ***Andy Blake in Advertising***. It became volume I of an eponymous four-book series.

It began life as a Canadian interactive Flash movie, but ***What's with Andy?*** became an animated TV series in 2001, featuring 'the world's greatest prankster' Andy Larkin.

Marvel Comics' Awesome Android first appeared in a 1963 instalment of the *Fantastic Four*. It was the creation of Stan Lee and a sidekick of the Mad Thinker character. By the time of his most recent appearance in 2005's *She-Hulk*, he had gained sentience and the new name **Awesome Andy**.

ANDREW CHARACTERS

Ricky Gervais played **Andy Millman** in *Extras*.

Woody Allen plays **Andrew Hobbs** in his 1982 movie *A Midsummer Night's Sex Comedy*.

Ewan McGregor plays **Andy** in the miner's strike/brass band Britflick *Brassed Off*.

Tim Robbins plays **Andy Dufresne** in the popular prison-break drama *The Shawshank Redemption*.

The toys Woody, Buzz, Slinky, Wheezy etc, in both *Toy Story* movies were owned by a boy called **Andy** (Davies).

The eponymous hero of *The 40-Year-Old Virgin*, played by Steve Carell, is a character called **Andy Stitzer**.

Jim Broadbent plays chef **Andy** in Mike Leigh's *Life is Sweet*. Dennis Franz played the central character of **Andy Sipowicz** in the hugely popular TV series *NYPD Blue*.

Andrew Trudeau in the series *Charmed* is portrayed by actor T. W. King.

———◆———

FUNNY ANDREWS

British audiences are likely to know him as the bewildered, multiple-personality Latka Gravas in the popular 1970s

US sitcom *Taxi*, or the subject of Jim Carrey's *Man on the Moon* biopic. But, although character acting brought him mass recognition, **Andy Kaufman** went his own way. An edgy, experimental and original performer, he disliked being called a comedian. He was so famously obsessed with faking his own death that some still believe he did so in 1984. Kaufman first made his name on *Saturday Night Live* when his performances included 'Foreign Man' – an embryo of Latka – and a startlingly funny Elvis impression.

His run ended after almost half a million viewers entered a 'Keep Andy/Dump Andy' phone poll. Kaufman had proposed the idea and promised to honour the verdict, which narrowly went against him. Although he stopped appearing on the show, some think this, too, was set up.

Of Kaufman's live performances, Carnegie Hall 1979 is perhaps the most notorious. Kaufman took the audience for milk and cookies after the show and invited them to join him the next morning, on the Staten Island Ferry, to see the remainder of the show. REM immortalised Kaufman with the song Man On The Moon on their 1992 album Automatic For The People.

A distinctively sardonic tone and a sharp, likeable sense of humour have made **Andy Hamilton** (b. 1954) a favourite among BBC Radio 4's comedy audience. With a background in writing for TV and radio, Hamilton has been a mostly invisible force.

His writing CV is vast, stretching from *Not The Nine O'clock News* in 1979 to the latest series of *The Armstrong and Miller Show*. In recent years, Hamilton has become one of the regulars of the UK comedy panel show circuit. He often appears on such shows as *Have I Got News For You* and *I'm Sorry I Haven't a Clue*.

Diminutive in stature (5ft 3ins.), Hamilton often trades 'shortist' insults on-air with thumb-sized Sandi Toksvig. Speaking of thumbs, Hamilton was born with, as he puts it, "one and a half thumbs on one hand, and half a thumb on the other". The half thumbs were removed in his infancy.

Another key Andrew of the British comedy circuit, **Andy Parsons** is one of the country's leading satirical stand-ups. He began his career as a legal clerk, which he describes as "crushingly tedious… but it did bring in a bit of money, which allowed me to focus on comedy writing".

Veteran of nine series of BBC Radio 2's *Parsons and Naylor's Pull-Out Section,* he is now a regular on *Mock The Week* and a familiar voice on Radio 4's *The News Quiz*.

If you're familiar with the hugely influential *The Daily Show with John Stewart*, you'll recognise John Oliver more than the 'other' half of his satirist partnership with **Andy Zaltzman**. Together they wrote Radio 4's *The Department* and *Political Animal*.

Zaltzman is also a regular writer for *Bremner, Bird and Fortune*. He is the brother of writer and podcaster Helen Zaltzman and the son of sculptor Zack Zaltzman.

When **Andrew 'Dice' Clay** (b. 1957) moved from teen movie and sitcom bit-parts to full stand-up comedy in the late 1980s, his new name soon acquired the weight and timbre of an obscene profanity. Born Andrew Clay Silverstein, he adopted the 'Dice' monicker and stage persona of the character he played in the 1986 movie *Pretty in Pink*, and was soon shocking TV and theatre audiences across the United States with his own brand of apparently racist, misogynistic humour.

One early routine involved rewording popular nursery rhymes to cause maximum offence. Initially his career was helped more than hindered by his controversial status. The publicity generated by his lifetime ban from MTV and other performers' refusals to appear in the same show, certainly raised his profile at first. However, Clay's alienation of various performing partners and agents has sometimes disastrously marginalised this comedian.

Writer, actor and comedian **Andrew Clover** (b.1970) is an Edinburgh Fringe regular who's appeared in a string of TV dramas and comedies including *Ashes to Ashes* (in which he played The Clown), *Cardiac Arrest*, *Casualty*, *Jonathan Creek* and *Gimme, Gimme, Gimme*.

He's the author of the kids' novel *Dirty Angels* and the brilliantly amusing guide to making fatherhood fun, *Dad*

Rules. Clover once appeared as a naked Morris dancer for Channel 4. He attended the European School of Luxembourg, and is embarrassed to recall linking arms with the Scandinavian children in playtime choruses of 'We won the war! In nineteen sixty-four!'

Ranting, misanthropic, fast-rising stand-up comedian **Andrew Lawrence** (b. 1980) combines a satanically deep voice with unusual looks ("If you stuck a bowtie on me, I'd look like a ventriloquist's dummy") and very dark humour.

His If.com Award-nominated 2006 Edinburgh Fringe show was called *How to Butcher Your Loved Ones*. Next year it was *Social Leprosy for Beginners and Improvers*.

His 2008 show was called *Don't Just Do Something, Sit There!* When asked recently to "tell us something we don't know about you", Lawrence revealed that he came third in the 1996 Surrey Schools Cross-Country Championships.

Emmy Award-winning US comedian **Andy Samberg** is a regular face on long-running staples *Saturday Night Live, Late Night with Conan O'Brien, The Daily Show with Jon Stewart* and *The Late Show with David Letterman*. He's a member of The Lonely Island comedy group and has made appearances on *Arrested Development*. He starred in *Hot Rod* (2007) and was one of the voices of *Space Chimps* (2008).

There are quite a few good stand-up Andrews on the comedy circuit. If you fancy laughing at (or ideally, with) an Andrew, try **Andrew O'Neill**, **Andy Borowitz** (US satirical writer/blogger who also penned *Fresh Prince of Bel Air*), **Andy Maxwell**, **Andy Smart**, **Andy Robinson**, **Andrew Watts** and **Andrew Roper** (Australian émigré).

<hr>

PIONEERING AND INVENTING ANDREWS

Though he's remembered for the make of car that bears his name, **André-Gustave Citroën** pioneered the use of double helical gears in an automobile.

During World War I he made armaments, founding his car company a year after it ended, in 1919. He died in Paris of stomach cancer in 1935.

Italian-born **Andrew Viterbi PhD.** is the electrical engineer and businessman behind some of the key technology in today's mobile phones and computers. His invention, the Viterbi algorithm, is used in cellular phones for error-correcting codes, in speech recognition and DNA analysis.

In the middle of the 18th century, **Andrew Planche** established the first china factory in Derby. He went into partnership with William Duesbury and opened a London showroom in 1773. The quality of the produce was recognised by George III who, in 1775, allowed the company to include a crown in its trademark. The company received its royal warrant from Queen Victoria in 1890. Crown Derby porcelain remains highly collectable.

The pastime of rolling down a hill, safely cushioned inside a large, soft plastic sphere comes from the land of extreme sports. New Zealander **Andrew Akers**, with co-conspirator Dwane van der Sluis, originally intended the double-skinned ball as an aquatic plaything.

They soon discovered that while it took a lot of human effort to get the Zorb moving on water, the merest breath of wind could scoot it out to sea. Much like its human originators, the idea crawled from the waves and adapted to life on land.

While many, including Leonardo da Vinci, could lay claim to having invented the parachute, **Andrew Garnerin** (1769-1823) is believed to be the first to have jumped with a frameless parachute (in 1797), and to have invented the air vent.

Before then, parachutes had rigid frames and no vents, making them cumbersome and relatively impractical. Vents keep the parachute steady as it falls; without them the air would spill from the sides, making it sway like a falling leaf.

Garnerin died after being hit by a beam while building a hot-air balloon. His wife, Jeanne-Geneviève, was the first female parachutist.

Like Andrew Garnerin, prolific inventor **Andrew Toti** (1915-2005) is not credited with the Big Idea in this case – that belongs to Peter Markus. But also like Garnerin, Toti perfected an existing concept and took it to market. His design for an inflatable life-jacket, with the vital addition of a crotch strap to prevent the wearer submarining, became the standard throughout the world. It was nicknamed the Mae West, after the buxom Hollywood actress of the time.

Writing in his later years, Dwight D. Eisenhower credited **Andrew Higgins** with having won World War II for the Allies. It was the famous Higgins boat, or LCVP (Landing Craft Vehicle, Personnel), that deposited the US troops on the Normandy beaches on D-Day. Without them, said Eisenhower; "We never could have landed over an open beach. The whole strategy of the war would have been different."

Not a million miles from the Mae West is **Andrew Zenoff's** maternity-minded invention. Few readers of this book, given the title, would benefit but new mothers around the world have Andrew to thank for a considerably more comfortable breast-feeding time. My Brest Friend is a soft, wraparound shelf-cum-backrest that provides a platform for the baby while also supporting the mother's lower back and arms.

Another improver, or perfecter. In **Andrew Moyer** we have not the discoverer of penicillin, but the man who increased its rate of production such that it became widely available when it was most needed. His work on mould nutrition in the early 1940s accelerated penicillin growth ten-fold, making it available and affordable following the immense flood of casualties following D-Day.

He was behind Polar Snow, a technology for making snow using a natural process in any temperature, but in the long run Australian inventor **Andrew French** (b. 1963) may be better remembered for Magnetic Drive.

This invention does away with gears and pulleys and uses magnetic force to create highly efficient, virtually frictionless motors. French also invented an escalator handrail that can display advertising, and an aquaculture system for Africa that raises fish stocks using rotten meat. The meat attracts flies whose maggots drop into the water, thereby attracting and feeding fish.

A truly extraordinary man, **Andrew J. Beard** was born into slavery in Woodland, Alabama in 1849. A farmer's son, his first two entries in the patent books were designs for ploughs. Later, as a railroad worker, he lost a leg in an accident while coupling two carriages.

His 1897 patent for the Jenny Coupler, which allowed carriages to couple automatically when brought together, undoubtedly saved many lives and even more limbs. The patent also made Beard very rich.

A series of patents for wire rope brought **Andrew Smith Hallidie** to his great invention, the cable car. San Francisco still uses his pioneering system of constantly moving underground cables to haul passenger cars along its streets.

Born Andrew Smith in 1836, he adopted the name Hallidie to honour his godfather, Sir Andrew Hallidie, who was William IV's and Queen Victoria's doctor.

It's an oddly British sight: a city gent in smart, dark pinstripes and Oxford shoes cycling along the bus lane beneath an incongruous, space-wedge helmet and atop a small-wheeled bicycle.

Invariably the chosen vehicle for these wealthy pedallers is the Brompton – a resolutely British brand of folding bicycle. Inventor **Andrew Ritchie** began his company in 1988 and remains MD of his still-private, and highly profitable, concern.

Poor (though not now in the financial sense) **Andrew Gordon** was laughed off the BBC series *Dragons' Den* when he tried to win backing for his Stabletable invention. A simple rubber wedge, The Stabletable is designed to stop four-legged furniture from wobbling, but Theo Paphitis thought it a solution to a problem already solved by free, established technology: folding a beer mat in half.

However, Gordon has proved the millionaires wrong, enjoying strong sales without their backing.

In the 1960s and 1970s, emerging computer companies put thousands of technicians to work developing uses for emerging solid-state 'Bubble' computer memory, invented by **Andrew H. Bobeck** (b. 1926) at AT & T Bell Laboratories in New Jersey, USA.

Bubble Memory uses no moving parts and looked like a promising replacement for magnetic tape and hard drives. However, it needed warm-up time and was slow to load and therefore not suitable for the high-performance market. The plunging cost of faster-access spinning hard drive technology through the 1980s consigned the invention to history.

There is some debate as to whether Scottish engineer **Andrew Meikle** (1719-1811) can be fully credited with the invention of the threshing machine – a contraption that greatly sped up the removal of the inedible outer husks from cereal grains – in the late 18th century.

He certainly produced what became the standard design for the revolutionary contraption, though some say he merely improved an existing design. Working as a millwright at Houston Mill in East Lothian, Meikle had previously invented the retractable, and therefore storm-proof, 'spring' windmill sail.

READ ALL ABOUT ANDREW

British-born, Irish-educated, US-based writer **Andrew Cockburn** (b. 1947) is the son of socialist author Claud Cockburn and the brother of fellow journalists Alexander and Patrick.

His half-sister is the mystery writer Sarah Caudwell. His half-brother-in-law was actor and broadcaster Michael Flanders (of Flanders and Swann). One of his daughters is actress Olivia Wilde.

Cockburn has co-written three books with his wife, the journalist and film producer Leslie Cockburn. His most recent tome is *Donald Rumsfeld: His Rise, Fall and Catastrophic Legacy* (2007).

Andrew Gilligan (b. 1968) is one of Britain's most prominent investigative journalists, whose comments and revelations become stories in themselves. His most notorious report for the BBC's *Today* programme concerned the "sexed up" Iraq dossier, which claimed Iraq could launch an attack with weapons of mass destruction within 45 minutes.

In the furore that surrounded the allegations that the Government "probably knew" this claim to be wrong, Gilligan revealed his source (Dr. David Kelly, who subsequently killed himself). The ensuing inquiries saw the BBC's Director-General Greg Dyke, its chairman Gavyn Davies and Gilligan himself losing their jobs.

In his new job at the *London Evening Standard*, Gilligan helped bring mayor Ken Livingstone's reign to an end by revealing that large, unaccounted sums of money were being paid by policing advisor Lee Jasper to friends and associates.

Andrew Marr (b. 1959) edited *The Independent* for two years between 1996 and 1998 (he was sacked for refusing to implement redundancies) and was the BBC's chief political editor for five years from 2000.

In the latter role he made his mark on the public consciousness with a lively, friendly style and is credited with having made dry parliamentary politics more approachable and interesting. He was represented on the impressionists' TV comedy show *Dead Ringers* with extraordinarily long, windmilling arms.

He quit BBC political reporting in 2005 and took over David Frost's vacated BBC1 Sunday morning interview slot, now called *The Andrew Marr Show*. In 2007 he wrote and presented a political history of post-war Britain on BBC2 – *Andrew Marr's History of Modern Britain* – and a year later produced the bird's eye documentary series *Britain from the Air*.

Dr. Andrew Mullen is senior lecturer in politics at Northumbria University in Newcastle-upon-Tyne and author of, among other book chapters and papers on politics, *The British Left's 'Great Debate' on Europe*.

Andrew Neil (b. 1949) was editor of *The Sunday Times* for 11 years. One notable scoop that brought down a former friend was the revelation that Conservative cabinet minister Cecil Parkinson – with whom Neil had once shared a flat – was having an extra-marital affair and had made his mistress pregnant.

During this time Neil was also founding chairman of Rupert Murdoch's Sky TV, overseeing its merger with BSB when it became British Sky Broadcasting. We have him to thank for first bringing *The Simpsons* to the UK.

Neil served as Lord Rector of the University of St Andrews from 1999 to 2002. In a running joke that still resurfaces from time to time, a particular shot of Neil standing in his vest beside a young Asian woman (with whom he once had a relationship) appears on the flimsiest excuses in the letters pages of *Private Eye*. Neil considers this racist.

Parliamentary sketch writer and broadcaster **Andrew Rawnsley** (b. 1962) is chief political commentator of *The Guardian*, and associate editor of *The Observer*. He was co-presenter of Channel 4's *A Week in Politics* and was until recently the presenter of BBC Radio 4's *The Westminster Hour*.

He now presents *The Sunday Edition* on ITV. He also wrote *Servants of the People* (2000) about New Labour's first years in power.

Historian and broadcaster **Andrew Roberts** (b. 1963) is heir to the British 'wing' of the Kentucky Fried Chicken empire. His biography of Lord Salisbury (*Salisbury: Victorian Titan*) won him the Wolfson History Prize and the James Stern silver pen award for non-fiction in 1999. He has written notably on the major political figures of the 20th century.

Andrew Roth (b. 1919) is the venerable and venerated compiler of the *Parliamentary Profiles*, the definitive published analyses of British MPs. Born in New York to Hungarian parents, he worked as a correspondent in many countries before settling in the UK in 1950.

In 1945, while working for US Naval Intelligence, he was arrested by the FBI in connection with leaked documents, but was cleared. He has written books on major British political figures such as Enoch Powell, Edward Heath, Harold Wilson and Tony Blair.

LITERARY ANDREWS

Britain's Poet Laureate from 1999 to 2009, **Andrew Motion** (b. 1952), is also a professor and award-winning biographer. He taught English at the University of Hull in the 1970s, was Professor of Creative Writing at UEA in the late 1980s and then occupied the same position at Royal Holloway, University of London.

He won the Somerset Maugham Award for *The Lamberts* in 1986 and the Whitbread Prize for Biography in 1999. As Poet Laureate, he has made his voice heard on various subjects, from celebrating Prince William's 21st birthday to condemning the invasion of Iraq. He spearheaded the online version of *The Poetry Archive* – a collection of live recordings of poets reading their own work.

Railwayman turned detective Jim Stringer, hero of *Death on a Branch Line*, *Murder at Deviation Junction*, *The Lost Luggage Porter* and a handful of other Edwardian track-based crime thrillers, is the creation of Yorkshire novelist **Andrew Martin**. A former barrister and journalist, Martin made his debut in the fictional world with comic northern novels *Bilton* and *The Bobby Dazzlers*.

One especially luminous figure in literary/scholarly circles as the 19th century became the 20th was the Scottish historian, critic and academician **Andrew Lang**. He's best known for *The Blue Book of Fairies*, a sumptuously produced and illustrated collection of fairy stories and one of many books he wrote on folklore, mythology and religion. His output was prodigious.

He published collections of French verses, had a broad career in journalism, was a literary editor, a pioneer in the new field of physic research, a Homeric scholar, an expert on the history of Scotland and the author of a bewildering range of books, papers, articles and essays. Lang is interred in the cathedral precincts at St. Andrews.

Blue plaque: '*Lang, Andrew (1844-1912), Man of Letters, lived here in 1876-1912*' at 1 Marloes Road, Kensington and Chelsea W8, 1959'.

There may be no more literary talent in the wine world than writer and broadcaster **Andrew Jefford** (b. 1956). The winner of eight Glenfiddich Awards and many other writing and broadcasting gongs, Jefford's work on food and drink reveals a real passion for writing about taste. He's written countless articles and more than 15 books.

A school friend and colleague of John Milton and a supporter of Oliver Cromwell, **Andrew Marvell** (1621-1678) was a satirical poet and parliamentarian who wrote stinging satire in an age when it was easy to lose your head.

After graduating from Cambridge, he became a tutor to children of the aristocracy, including the daughter of Lord General Fairfax and the ward of Cromwell himself. Marvell saved Milton from execution at the hands of Charles II at least once, and wrote a poem to preface the second edition of Milton's *Paradise Lost*. At the time of his death in 1678 he was MP for Hull.

Glaswegian **Andrew O'Hagan**'s first novel, *Our Fathers*, was shortlisted for the Booker and Whitbread prizes; his second, *Personality*, won the James Tait Black Memorial Prize for fiction. A film critic for *Esquire* magazine and occasional journalist, O'Hagan is also a Goodwill Ambassador for the UK branch of Unicef.

One of the most highly regarded histories of Scotland from the Middle Ages is the 14th century rhyming *Chronicle* by **Andrew Wyntown**. Without once breaking rhythm, Wyntown rattles through all extant Scottish history without feeling it necessary to distinguish between myth and actuality. His exact dates are unknown.

Reformed hooligan **Andrew Nicholls** could equally well figure in the Criminals section. But, he's the author of four books on football violence, including a two-part encyclopaedia called *Hooligans: the A-L [&M-Z] of Britain's Football Gangs*, and *30 Years of Hurt: A History of England's Hooligan Army*.

He's under a lifetime ban from the club he follows, Everton, and must remain 10 miles from any football ground where they're playing. He was once banned from every ground in England and Wales. He has said that the only way to stop football hooliganism was to amputate the arms and legs of every male fan between 14 and 40 years old.

If the unofficial national anthem of Australia is Waltzing Matilda, its favourite poem is *The Man From Snowy River*. Both are bush poems by **Andrew Barton "Banjo" Paterson**. Banjo (a pseudonym he took from his favourite horse) wrote the latter in 1890, and the book of works compiled under the same title five years later is still a best-seller.

Banjo became a journalist during the Second Boer War, and was an ambulance driver during World War I.

A Nobel Prize winner four years before his death in 1951, Frenchman **André Gide's** writing included both fiction and autobiography. He was a friend of Oscar Wilde (who believed he had 'turned' Gide gay, though the latter had already confirmed his sexuality).

He married his cousin, but did not consummate the marriage and eventually eloped with the son of his best man. His wife burned his letters, much to his dismay as he considered them his best work. He eventually conceived a daughter, Catherine, in a one-off encounter with the daughter of his friend, the Belgian neo-impressionist painter Théo van Rysselberghe.

Gide published more than 80 works in his life, including *L'immoraliste* (1902), *Le retour de l'enfant prodigue* (1907), *Corydon* (1920) and *Si le grain ne meurt* (1926 – autobiography).

Russian novelist **Andrei Bely** is mainly known for his 1913 novel *Petersburg*. Bely was the nom de plume of Boris Nikolaevich Bugaev. The unsettling symbolist masterpiece, one of almost 30 published works by Bugaev, is thought to be a forerunner to James Joyce's *Ulysses*. Though there are broad similarities, it was not translated into English until 1959, so Joyce was no plagiarist.

Born in Istanbul, **Andrew Mango** was based in London for most of his career. He worked in the BBC's External Services, culminating in the role of Turkish Programme Organiser. But he has made his mark on the non-fiction world since retirement. Most notably, he wrote *Atatürk: The Biography of the Founder of Modern Turkey*, which has become the recognised authority on the man who rebuilt Turkey after World War I.

Born in Panama and raised in Jamaica, **Andrew Salkey** was among the first wave of Caribbean writers to gain prominence on the London literary scene. For some time Salkey was the presenter and writer-in-residence in the Caribbean section of the BBC *World Service*.

He wrote a number of novels, including works for children, and edited anthologies of upcoming Caribbean writers. His best known works are *A Quality of Violence* (1959), *Stories from the Caribbean* (1965) and *Anancy's Score* (1973) (Anancy is a figure in popular Caribbean folklore akin to Br'er Rabbit). Salkey died in the USA in 1995.

Novelist **Andrew Taylor** (b. 1951) is behind a string of popular crime novels and series including the Dougal series, the Lydmouth series and the Roth Trilogy. He also wrote the best-selling *The American Boy*. He has twice won the Crime Writers' Association's Historical Dagger award, a unique achievement. Taylor has also written a string of *Bergerac* novels, under the pseudonym Andrew Saville.

Bravo Two Zero is the best-selling war book of all time. Written by former SAS commando **Andy McNab**, it describes a failed operation during the first Gulf War. It has sold more than 1.7 million copies in 16 languages.

McNab is a pseudonym; the author always appears in shadow or silhouette on screen to conceal his identity from terrorist groups. Before he retired from the services, McNab was the military's most decorated soldier.

Andrew Scott Berg is the author of a small number of acclaimed biographies. His first, *Maxwell Perkins: Editor of Genius* (1978), won him a National Book Award. A Guggenheim Fellowship helped finance his second work, *Goldwyn: A Biography* (about MGM producer Samuel Goldwyn, published in 1989).

His third, *Lindbergh*, (1998) was a *New York Times* Best Seller and won the Pulitzer Prize. *Kate Remembered*, about Berg's long friendship with Katherine Hepburn, arrived in 2003 within days of the actress's death.

⋙◆⋘

MILITARY ANDREWS

In 1893, at the age of 10, Andrew Cunningham received a telegram from his father asking if he would like to go join the navy. Cunningham had shown no particular interest and the family had no maritime background, but after some thought he sent the reply: "Yes, I should like to be an admiral."

At the north end of London's Trafalgar Square, the busts of three First Sea Lords gaze out across the expanse. Among them is **Admiral of the Fleet Andrew Cunningham**, 1st Viscount Cunningham of Hyndhope, Bt (Baronetcy), KT (Knight of the Thistle), GCB (Knight Grand Cross of the Order of the Bath), OM (Order of Merit), DSO** (Distinguished Service Order, with two bars). His many other military honours included the Special Grand Cordon of the Cloud and Banner (from China), the Legion d'honneur, Commandeur (France) and Grand Cordon of the Order of Nichan Iftikhar (Tunisia).

Cunningham commanded a destroyer during the first war, earning his DSO and its enhancements from the Dardanelles and Baltic campaigns. In World War II, as Commander-in-Chief of the Mediterranean fleet,

Cunningham scored several important victories while controlling the defence of the supply lines.

He became First Sea Lord in 1943 and remained the most senior officer in the Royal Navy until his retirement in 1946. General D Eisenhower, Supreme Commander of the Allied Forces, said of Cunningham: "He remains in my opinion at the top of my subordinates in absolute selflessness, energy, devotion to duty, knowledge of his task, and in understanding of the requirements of allied operations." Andrew Cunningham died in 1963.

Andrew Jackson Smith made his name during the American Civil War, in particular for forcing Confederate General Nathan Bedford Forrest's force into its worst defeat of the war, at the Battle of Tupelo, Mississippi, on July 14th 1864.

Another Union soldier, African-American Corporal **Andrew Jackson Smith**, won the country's highest military decoration – the Medal of Honour – for his bravery during the Battle of Honey Hill. The citation reads:

"Forced into a narrow gorge crossing a swamp in the face of the enemy position, the 55th's Colour-Sergeant was killed by an exploding shell, and Corporal Smith took the Regimental Colours from his hand and carried them through heavy grape and canister fire. Although half of the officers and a third of the enlisted men engaged in the fight were killed or wounded, Corporal Smith continued to expose himself to enemy fire by carrying the colours throughout the battle. Through his actions, the Regimental Colours of the 55th Infantry Regiment were not lost to the enemy."

General Andrew McNaughton, CH, CB, CMG, DSO, CD, PC (1887-1966) was a Canadian officer and politician who led the Canadian army into World War II. He was blamed for the disastrous Dieppe Raid in 1942. His grandson, **Lt.-General Andrew Leslie** CMM, MSC, MSM, CD, is the Chief of the Land Staff of the Canadian Forces.

The highest ranking Scottish seaman at the close of the 15th century was **Sir Andrew Wood of Largo**, Lord High Admiral of Scotland. He served under James III and James IV, beginning as a merchant and rising rapidly through the ranks as his fleet and influence grew.

He fought a fierce and lengthy sea battle with English admiral Stephen Bull in the Firth of Forth off Edinburgh. Outnumbered in both ships and guns, Wood was nevertheless victorious and captured all the English ships. He was knighted by James IV in about 1495.

A contemporary of Wood's, **Sir Andrew Barton**, was also a High Admiral of Scotland.

Notorious in England and Portugal as a pirate, Barton operated under the aegis of a letter of marque (official

warrant or commission) on behalf of the Scottish crown,
and was therefore more accurately described as a privateer.
He was defeated, captured and killed in 1511 by Sir
Edward Howard.

***

MUSICAL ANDREWS

Here's an album that should be on the shelves of every
Andrew who can find it. Recorded by Andrew Hill on Blue
Note Records and released in 1968, it's a jazz number with
the fabulous title: **Andrew!!!**

Frank Zappa recorded a track called **Andy** on his album
One Size Fits All (1975).

The Killers recorded a song called **Andy, You're A Star**
on their 2005 album Hot Fuss.

David Bowie wrote the song **Andy Warhol** for his 1971
album Hunky Dory.

The Cranberries' 2002 album Treasure Box includes the
song **Desperate Andy**.

The Indigo Girls' 1999 Come On Now Social album
includes a song called **Andy**.

Tammany Hall Nyc's Back in the Bottle finishes with the
song **Andy Climb Down**.

Baron Lloyd-Webber (b. 1948), better known sans hyphen as **Andrew Lloyd Webber**, is one of the most successful composers of all time – certainly in terms of popularity and wealth. His 1980s work established him as the king of musical theatre with hits including *Joseph and the Amazing Technicolor Dreamcoat*, *Jesus Christ Superstar*, *Evita*, *Cats*, *Starlight Express* and *Phantom of the Opera*.

The latter – which premiered in 1986 – is still running in the West End and on Broadway. Of his 1980s' productions, only *Aspects of Love* enjoyed limited success, not even lasting a full year on Broadway.

Soon after the turn of the decade, Lloyd Webber launched *Sunset Boulevard*, possibly the most expensive musical ever staged. Although popular, it lost money in London and especially New York, where 25-million-dollar losses made it the biggest financial failure ever recorded in the business.

The following string of musicals did not fare much better and it seemed Lloyd Webber's star had waned… until in recent years he reinvented himself as a TV talent show impresario. It all began with *How Do You Solve a Problem Like Maria* (to cast the lead in *The Sound of Music*), through *Any Dream Will Do* (*Joseph*) to his latest casting telethon, *I'll Do Anything* (*Oliver!* – mainly for the part of Nancy, but also the title role).

Since his first published pieces at the age of nine, he has raised and donated a phenomenal amount of money to charity, and still has problems with the cat that managed to delete work from his computer.

He currently owns seven London theatres and was knighted in 1992, becoming a life peer in 1997.

They recorded more than 700 songs and had nine gold discs. They were the first all-female group to 'go platinum'. They sold more than 90 million records, and had 46 songs in the Billboard American Top 10, and were for many Americans the defining sound of World War II radio.

And they didn't just sing; they appeared in radio series, commercials, Hollywood movies and on Broadway. They were The **Andrews Sisters** – Patty, Maxene and LaVerne – America's most popular female singing group.

The German-born, Academy and Grammy Award-winning pianist, conductor and composer **André Previn** first came to prominence for work on Hollywood film scores in the late 1940s.

In a career packed with superlatives, Previn has won four Oscars (he has scored at least a dozen movies and three Broadway shows), is an honourary Knight of the British Empire (KBE) and was recently awarded the 2008 Gramaphone Lifetime Achievement Award.

He has recorded just about every major classical work, conducted the world's greatest orchestras and played classical and jazz piano around the globe. He's been married five times and is Woody Allen's father-in-law, after the director's marriage to Previn's adopted daughter Soon Yi.

His most famous appearance for British audiences, though, was on the *Morecambe and Wise* show in 1971. In one of the nation's favourite comedy moments, he kept an admirably straight face while Morecambe held him by the lapels and muttered that he was "playing all the right notes, just not necessarily in the right order".

Better known as **André 3000** (b. 1975), André Lauren Benjamin is an American musician and actor, best known for his work in the group OutKast. Mr. 3000 has appeared in a handful of recent films, including in *Be Cool*, *Four Brothers*, *Idlewild*, *Revolver*, *Charlotte's Web* (voice), *Semi-Pro* and *Battle in Seattle*.

He owns his own production company – Moxie Turtle – which, among other things, makes his Emmy Award-winning *Class of 3000* animated comedy series. He was awarded World's Sexiest Vegetarian Celebrity (male) by PETA in 2004.

Violin, mandolin, guitar and glockenspiel-playing **Andrew Bird** is a Chicago-based singer-songwriter. His latest of eight albums is Armchair Apocrypha (2007), on the Fat Possum label.

Canadian singer-songwriter **Andrew Cash** recorded with the bands L'Etranger and Ursula before going solo. He made an album with his brother, Peter, called The Cash Brothers, and released another solo album, Murder, in 2007.

British conductor **Sir Andrew Davis CBE** has been associate conductor of the BBC Scottish Symphony Orchestra, principal conductor with the Toronto Symphony Orchestra, music director at Glyndebourne, chief conductor of the BBC Symphony Orchestra and was music director and principal conductor of the Lyric Opera, Chicago.

He conducted the Prom at the Palace for the Queen's 2002 Golden Jubilee and is associated with British composer Michael Tippet, whose works he has debuted.

Sisters of Mercy frontman **Andrew Eldritch** (born Andrew Taylor in 1959 and also known – when on the drum machine – as Doktor Avalanche) is the sole surviving original member of his band.

Even when it was still together, the goth-reinventing group saw nine members fly in and out of its revolving doors, and feuds with former colleagues peppered the music press for years. A dispute with his record company over contractual obligations prompted Eldritch to refuse to lay down any more tracks.

An album called SSV (Screw Shareholder Value), which wasn't released, finally persuaded EastWest Records to give up on expecting more.

Classical composer **Andrew Glover**'s music has been performed by the BBC Symphony Orchestra, the English

Northern Philharmonic and The Latin American String Quartet, among others.

Born in 1962, he has written pieces in various classical and jazz genres from solo instruments to full symphony orchestra, his most well known works being Fractured Vistas for Orchestra and The Fickle Virgin of Seventeen Summers. He has recently completed his piano concerto The Time of Moments.

Andrew Jackson Jihad is a controversial Phoenix, Arizona, rock group – a collective of visiting musicians around the core duo of Sean Bonnette and Ben Gallant. Many of the lyrics are political, and the albums and tracks sometimes bear memorable names, such as People That Can Eat People Are the Luckiest People in the World (2007) and Only God Can Judge Me, on Plan-It-X Records (2008).

Andrew Lewis is an 'acousmatic' composer – a classical composer who arranges the sounds of instruments and (especially in Lewis's case) ambient noises from the environment into a recorded composition.

As professor of music at Bangor University he was heavily influenced by the surrounding landscape. Ascent (1994), relating to the soundscape of Snowdonia, was awarded a 'Euphonie d'Or' by the Bourges electroacoustic music competition.

He's the singer, pianist and songwriter behind the band Something Corporate and solo project Jack's Mannequin, but American musician **Andrew McMahon** will be forever linked with the fight against leukaemia.

He suddenly cancelled a string of gigs after being diagnosed with acute lymphoblastic leukaemia in 2005. His ongoing and publicly fought battle with the disease, including the news of his stem-cell transplant from sister Katie, raised thousands of pounds for the Pediatric Cancer Research Foundation.

In 2006, after announcing the end of his course of treatment, McMahon founded The Dear Jack Foundation to raise funds for cancer research.

Andrew Ridgeley (b. 1963) is the other 'half' (with George Michael) of Eighties pop superduo Wham!. The pair met at school, landed a recording deal on the strength of a hurriedly put-together demo tape, and had massive success in four short years between 1982 and 1986.

After Wham! split, Ridgeley moved to Monaco to try motor racing, and then to Los Angeles to become an actor. Neither quite took off. On his 1990 return to the UK he recorded one contractually-obligated solo album – *Son of Albert* – and then retired from music making.

Ridgeley has become something of an environmentalist since contracting an illness from raw sewage while surfing, and supports clean-water organisations. He is married to Keren Woodward, of Bananarama. He seems the likely inspiration for The Andrew Ridgeleys, a rock band from Iowa.

Andrew Stockdale is an Australian photographer-turned-musician best known as the singer/guitarist of Wolfmother.

Classical American pianist **Andrew von Oeyen** made his performance debut in 1985, aged 16, with the Los Angeles Philharmonic. He has since appeared as a soloist with many world-class orchestras.

Von Oeyen was the 1999 recipient of the prestigious Gilmore Young Artist Award and won First Prize in the Lení Fé Bland Foundation National Competition in 2001.

Andrew W. K. is on a mission to party, in a non-stop guitar-thrashing, hair-whipping frenzy. The son of a prominent legal scholar, California-born Andrew Wilkes-Krier trained on the piano from an early age and was a member of countless bands before going solo in 2001.

His tracks tend to appear in video games aimed at teenage boys.

In the second season of *X-Factor*, Shane Ward was just too young and good-looking for co-finalist **Andy Abraham**. A refuse collector in his 40s, Andy was a diamond in the rough, with good singing technique and Nat King Cole's warm tones. His first album, The Impossible Dream, went platinum with 300,000+ sales. In 2008, he represented the UK in the Eurovision Song Contest.

Much to Terry Wogan's frustration, he came last.

In 1990, Mother Love Bone's flamboyant frontman and songwriter **Andrew Wood** died aged 24 from a heroin overdose, departing a promising-looking musical career in the early days of grunge.

Two members of his band went on to form Pearl Jam, and various contemporaries have paid tribute to him in song, notably Eddie Vedder, Warrant, Alice in Chains and The Cult. The Scott Barbour documentary *Malfunkshun: The Andrew Wood Story* was released in 2005.

Andy was the Gibb who never quite joined the band. A decade or so younger than Robin, Barry and Maurice, **Andy Gibb** (b.1958) lived in the shadow of the Bee Gees, despite having considerable personal success as a musician and recording artist.

He was the first male solo artist with three consecutive top spots in the US Billboard charts – the second of which knocked his brothers' Stayin' Alive off the top spot. His first album Flowing Rivers sold more than a million copies. The title track of his second album, Shadow Dancing (which is credited to all four brothers) went platinum after seven weeks at number one.

But, thanks to drug misuse, it was the beginning of the end. He was fired from the cast of both shows and from his relationship with *Dallas* star Victoria Principal. He toured extensively through the latter part of the 1980s but was eventually declared bankrupt. He had won a new recording contract in the UK when, soon after his 30th birthday in 1988, he died from an inflamed heart.

Cocaine can do that.

Andrew Russo shares his name with one of the mobsters in our Naughty Andrews section, but this one is an American solo pianist. Russo has released a series of American composer portraits, including John Corigliano's piano and chamber works and Steve Reich's Piano Phase as well as US premieres of works by Holland's Jacob ter Veldhuis and Gerard Beljon, the French premiere of Crumb's *Eine Kleine Mitternachtmusik*, and world premieres of works written for Russo by American composers Derek Bermel and Marc Mellits and British composer James Aitchison.

Russo also dedicates time to the direction and development of Music Journeys INC, a non-profit foundation he founded in 2001. His latest album, Mix Tape (2008), features piano solo interpretations of such radically diverse songs as You're Beautiful, All Tomorrow's Parties and Play That Funky Music, White Boy.

US-based Armenian-Iranian singer-songwriter Andranik Madadian, better known by his stage name, **Andy**, is probably the most successful pop artist in Persian music history. His early albums with performer Kouros, released in the late 1980s, were huge hits (in particular Balla!). Andy went solo in 1992 and has since released 15 albums and has been awarded Best Armenian International Singer of the year four times.

Since 2000, proudly Mancunian band Oasis have had a southerner in their midst. Although he was no bassist, when the Gallagher brothers heard that songwriter-guitarist **Andy Bell** (b. 1970) was available for work, they snatched him from the jaws of another band and offered him the job.

His arrival forced a loosening up of roles. Although he had to learn the bass part for the band's back catalogue at short notice, Bell plays guitar on the tracks he wrote himself.

In 1985 Vince Clark, co-founder of Depeche Mode and Yazoo, advertised in the paper for a singer for his next project. Meat packer **Andy Bell** (b. 1964) was chosen from among the many that auditioned. As Erasure, they went on to sell more than 20 million albums and had 24 consecutive Top 20 hits in the UK.

Among his projects outside Erasure, Bell appeared on the 1990 Red Hot + Blue album to raise funds for Aids and HIV research, and sang the role of Montresor in Peter Hammill's opera *The Fall of the House of Usher* in 1991.

In 2005, Bell released his first solo album, Electric Blue, a year after announcing that he was HIV-positive.

Andy Irvine is a singer, songwriter and a founding member of Christy Moore's popular Irish band Planxty. He plays mandolin, bouzouki, mandola and guitar-bouzouki.

Jazz pianist, composer, and arranger **Andy LaVerne** has worked with some of the jazz greats, including Frank Sinatra, Stan Getz, Woody Herman, Dizzy Gillespie, Chick Corea and Lionel Hampton.

He has appeared as band leader on more than 50 albums. LaVerne has also released a series of instructional videos, books and play-along CD/books. He is the recipient of five Jazz Fellowships from the National Endowment for the Arts. He won the 2000 John Lennon Songwriting contest for his tune Shania.

Andy Scott plays lead guitar with the 1970s glam rock band Sweet, best remembered for their string of 1973 hits including Ballroom Blitz, Wig Wam Bam and Block Buster (which topped the charts). He is the longest-serving band member and still tours with Sweet in Germany, where the band was especially popular, scoring eight number one hits.

Andy White is a Belfast-born singer/songwriter and poet. He released his first of 13 albums, Rave on Andy White, in

1986. He has collaborated with Peter Gabriel and Sinéad O'Connor. White is best known for songs such as James Joyce's Grave and Street Scenes From My Heart.

Mr. Moon River, **Andy Williams** (b. 1927) has recorded 18 gold and three platinum albums. He has performed with, well, everyone. He had his own popular TV variety show from 1962 to 1971 and built his own 2,000-seater stadium, the Moon River Theatre, in Branson, Missouri.

He had produced so many timelessly elegant, signature recordings of great songs that they hit the charts again almost every time they resurface in advertising. His 1967 recording of Music to Watch Girls By reached number nine in the UK on the back of a Fiat Punto ad.

His 1963 recording of It's The Most Wonderful Time Of The Year reached 21 in December 2007 thanks to a Marks & Spencer ad. Williams was close friends with Robert F. Kennedy and was present at the Ambassador Hotel when RFK was assassinated in June 1968.

Californians have him to thank for the letter W in the Hollywood sign. He was the sponsor of the letter during the sign's 1987 restoration.

Andy Summers is best known as the guitarist with The Police. The band produced six albums between 1978 and 1983 before splitting up. Since then Summers has released 14 solo albums in an eclectic range of styles, including

Green Chimneys – The Music of Thelonius Monk in 1999, and albums with Robert Fripp, John Etheridge, Victor Biglione and most recently Ben Verdery.

Summers' credits include film scores for *Down and Out in Beverly Hills* and *Weekend at Bernie's*. His playing has been influenced by years of jazz and classical music studies, as well as new age, rock, and other musical genres. The Police reunited for a highly successful world tour in 2007.

Guitarist **Andy Taylor** (b. 1961) was most famously a member of Duran Duran, the definitive and hugely successful New Romantic boy band of the 1980s. He was also a member of The Power Station, a band formed with singer Robert Palmer during a break in Duran Duran's recording schedule.

He played on many of Palmer's hits, including the most famous – Addicted To Love – from 1985. As a guitarist, Taylor had a harder edge to his musical taste than the synth-based music of mid-1980s Duran Duran.

The recording of the album Notorious saw Duran Duran hanging on to Taylor by their fingernails. He played on few tracks, but his subsequent 'temporary' departure was to last 15 years. He concentrated on a solo career before turning to full-time producing only rejoining Duran Duran for their original-lineup reunion in 2000. Taylor now owns his own studios in Ibiza, and sells unsigned artists in MP3 format via the internet.

NOBEL & IGNOBEL

Nobel Prize winners - Medicine

London-born **Sir Andrew F. Huxley** (b. 1917), OM, FRS, won the 1963 Nobel Prize for Physiology or Medicine (shared with research partner Alan Hodgkin and John Eccles) for his work on the electrical impulses that enable physical activity to be co-ordinated by a central nervous system.

Thought to be one of the world's greatest mathematical biologists, Huxley was knighted in 1974 and appointed to the Order of Merit in 1983. He comes from a most illustrious family. He is the grandson of biologist T. H. Huxley, son of the writer Leonard Huxley and half-brother of the writer Aldous Huxley and fellow biologist Julian Huxley.

He is also the grandson-in-law of Josiah Wedgewood.

The 2006 Prize was awarded to **Andrew Fire** (b. 1959) and Craig C. Mello for the discovery of RNA interference, which has revolutionised our understanding of genetic management. Fire is a professor of pathology and genetics at Stanford University School of Medicine in the USA.

French microbiologist **André Lwoff**, who died in 1994 aged 92, won the 1965 Nobel Prize in Medicine for his research into viral infections of bacteria. Lwoff worked almost throughout the 20th century on viral research, making significant strides into the understanding of the poliovirus.

The 1956 Nobel Prize in Physiology or Medicine was awarded to **André Cournand** (with Werner Forssmann and Dickinson W. Richards) for 'discoveries concerning heart catheterisation and pathological changes in the circulatory system' (from the Nobel citation).

French-born Cournand was a professor at the College of Physicians and Surgeons of Columbia University.

Polish endocrinologist (specialist in the hormone system) **Andrzej Schally** was educated in the UK before leaving for a research post in the US. He won the 1977 Nobel Prize in medicine for his work in birth control methods and growth hormones.

Peace

Andrei Sakharov was unable to collect his Nobel Peace Prize in 1975. His wife read his acceptance speech in Oslo. Following the publication of his treatise against anti-ballistic missile defence (a crucial Soviet-US issue in the late 1960s) the eminent nuclear physicist and human rights activist had been banned by the Russian government from working on military projects or leaving the country.

Literature

André Gide won the 1947 Nobel Prize for Literature for his "comprehensive and artistically significant writings, in which human problems and conditions have been presented with a fearless love of truth and keen psychological insight".

There's more on Gide in the Literary Andrews section.

IgNobel

The 1996 IgNobel award for medicine went to James Johnston of R J Reynolds, Joseph Taddeo of US Tobacco, **Andrew Tisch** of Lorillard, William Campbell of Philip Morris, Edward Horrigan of Liggett Group, Donald Johnston of American Tobacco Company, and the late Thomas Sandefur Jr., chairman of Brown and Williamson Tobacco Co; for their discovery (as testified to the US Congress) that nicotine is not addictive.

———◆———

OLYMPIC & PARALYMPIC MEDAL-WINNING ANDREWS SINCE **1924**

Andrew Charlton (Australia) Swimming
Paris 1924: 1500m freestyle, Bronze; 400m freestyle, Bronze
Amsterdam 1928: 1500m freestyle, Silver; 400m freestyle, Silver

Andrew MacDonald (Great Britain) Wrestling
Freestyle
Paris 1924: + 87kg (heavyweight), Bronze

Andrew J. Libano Jr. (United States) Sailing
Los Angeles 1932: two-person keelboat open (Star Mixed), Gold

Andrew Stanfield (United States) Athletics
Helsinki 1952: 200m, Gold; 4 x 100m relay, Gold
Melbourne 1956: 200m, Silver

Mark Andrew Spitz (United States) Swimming
Mexico 1968: 100m butterfly, Silver; 100m freestyle, Bronze;
4x100m freestyle relay, Gold; 4 x 200m freestyle relay, Gold
Munich 1972: 100m butterfly, Gold; 100m freestyle, Gold;
200m butterfly, Gold;
200m freestyle, Gold; 4 x 100m freestyle relay, Gold; 4 x
100m medley relay, Gold; 4 x 200m freestyle relay, Gold

David Andrew Wilkie (Great Britain) Swimming
Munich 1972: 200m breaststroke, Silver
Montreal 1976: 100m breaststroke, Silver; 200m breaststroke, Gold

Andrew Justice (Great Britain) Rowing
Moscow 1980: eight with coxswain (8+), Silver

Andrew Weaver (United States) Cycling (Road)
Los Angeles 1984: team time trial, Bronze

Andrew Sudduth (United States) Rowing
Los Angeles 1984: eight with coxswain (8+), Silver

Andrew Holmes (Great Britain) Rowing
Los Angeles 1984: four-oared shell with coxswain, Gold
Seoul 1988: coxless pair, Gold; pair-oared shell with
coxswain, Bronze

Andrew Astbury (Great Britain) Swimming
Los Angeles 1984: 4 x 200m freestyle relay, Bronze

Andrew J. McDonald (United States) Water polo
Los Angeles 1984: water polo, Silver

Andrew Rein (United States) Wrestling Freestyle
Los Angeles 1984: 62-68kg (lightweight), Silver

Andrew Maynard (United States) Boxing
Seoul 1988: 75-81kg (light-heavyweight), Gold

Andrew Bennie (New Zealand) Equestrian/Eventing
Seoul 1988: team (mixed), Bronze

Andrew Bird (New Zealand) Rowing
Seoul 1988: four-oared shell with coxswain, Bronze

Andrew Jameson (Great Britain) Swimming
Seoul 1988: 100m butterfly, Bronze

Andrew Valmon (United States) Athletics
Barcelona 1992: 4 x 400m relay, Gold

Andrew Hoy (Australia) Equestrian/Eventing
Barcelona 1992: team (mixed), Gold
Atlanta 1996: team (mixed), Gold
Sydney 2000: individual (mixed), Silver; team (mixed), Gold

Andrew Nicholson (New Zealand) Equestrian/Eventing
Barcelona 1992: team (mixed), Silver
Atlanta 1996: team (mixed), Bronze

Andrew Crosby (Canada) Rowing
Barcelona 1992: eight with coxswain (8+), Gold

Andrew Cooper (Australia) Rowing
Barcelona 1992: four without coxswain (4-), Gold

Andrew Gabel (United States) Short Track Speed Skating
Lillehammer 1994: 5000m relay, Silver

Andrew Murtha (Australia) Short Track Speed Skating
Lillehammer 1994:5000m relay, Bronze

Andrew Trim (Australia) Canoe/Kayak Flatwater
Atlanta 1996: K-2 500m (kayak double), Bronze
Sydney 2000: K-2 500m (kayak double), Silver

Andrew Landenberger (Australia) Sailing
Atlanta 1996: tornado – (multihull mixed), Silver

Andrew Lindsay (Great Britain) Rowing
Sydney 2000: eight with coxswain (8+), Gold

Andrew Rock (Australia) Athletics
Athens 2004: 4 x 400m relay, Silver

Andrew Utting (Australia) Baseball
Athens 2004: Silver

Andrew Triggs Hodge (Great Britain) Rowing
Beijing 2008: (fours), Gold

Andrew Simpson (Great Britain) Sailing
Beijing 2008: star class, Gold

Andrew Lauterstein (Australia) Swimming
Beijing 2008: 4 x 100m freestyle relay, Bronze; 100m
butterfly, Bronze; 4 x 100m medley, Silver

Andrew Smith (Australia) Hockey
Beijing 2008: men's tournament, Bronze

PARALYMPIANS

Andrew Gilbert (Great Britain) Swimming
Stoke Mandeville/NY 1984: 100m freestyle L4, Bronze; 100m
freestyle L4, Bronze; 400m freestyle L4, Bronze; 100m
backstroke L4, Silver
Seoul 1988: 100m freestyle L4, Bronze; 400m freestyle L4,
Bronze; 100m backstroke L4, Silver

Andrew Blake (Great Britain) Swimming
Seoul 1988: 50m Freestyle 3, Gold

Andrew O'Sullivan (Australia) Athletics
Seoul 1988: 400m A4/A9, Bronze; 4 x 400m relay A2/A4-7,
Gold

Andrew Parr (United States) Alpine Skiing
Salt Lake City 2002: giant slalom B3, Bronze; slalom B3, Silver

Andrew James Scott (Rhodesia) Swimming
Tel Aviv 1968: 50m breaststroke class 4 incomplete, Gold;

50m backstroke class 4 incomplete, Silver
Heidelberg 1972: 50m breaststroke 4, Bronze; 3 x 25m
medley 4, Gold; 50m backstroke 4, Silver
Arnhem 1980: 50m backstroke 3, Bronze

Andrew Blake (Great Britain) Wheelchair Basketball
Athens 2004: Bronze

Andrew Curtis (Great Britain) Athletics
Barcelona 1992: 4 x 100m relay B1>B3, Silver; 4 x 400m
relay B1>B3, Silver
Atlanta 1996: 100m T10, Bronze; 200m T10, Silver

Andrew Flavel (Australia) Wheelchair Basketball
Athens 2004: Silver

Andrew Haley (Canada) Swimming
Barcelona 1992: 400m freestyle S9, Bronze
Sydney 2000: 100m butterfly S9, Bronze; 400m freestyle S9,
Bronze

Andrew Lindsay (Great Britain) Swimming
Atlanta 1996: 100m backstroke S7, Silver
Sydney 2000: 100m backstroke S7, Gold
Athens 2004: 100m backstroke S7, Gold

Andrew Newell (Australia) Athletics
Sydney 2000: 100m T20, Bronze; 400m T20, Bronze

Andrew Panazzolo (Australia) Cycling Track
Athens 2004: individual pursuit bicycle CP Div 3, Bronze;
cycling track 1km time trial bicycle CP Div ¾, Silver

Andrew Parr (United States) Alpine Skiing
Salt Lake City 2002: giant slalom B3, Bronze; slalom B3, Silver

Andrew Slater (United States) Cycling Track
Sydney 2000: 1km time trial tandem open, Silver

Andrew Stubbs (Great Britain) Swimming
Barcelona 1992: 4 x 50m freestyle S1-6, Bronze

Andrew Yohe (United States) Ice Sledge Hockey
Turin 2006: Bronze

Andrew Hodge (Great Britain) Athletics
Barcelona 2002: 100 TW2, Gold

POLITICAL ANDREWS

Prime Ministers and Presidents

One of only two London blue plaques (the 'someone famous lived here' sign – the other is Andrew Lang, in the Literary Andrews section) bearing the name Andrew, at 24 Onslow Gardens, Kensington, commemorates the home of British Prime Minister **Andrew Bonar Law** (b. 1858).

Canadian Bonar Law himself was unique in being the only British PM to have been born outside the British Isles. He was also Britain's shortest serving Prime Minister, his term lasting only seven months.

Already a successful businessman by his mid-30s, Bonar Law won his first Conservative seat in Glasgow in 1900. Following the 1911 resignation of Arthur Balfour and subsequent stalemate between contenders Austen Chamberlain and Walter Long, Bonar Law was invited to become leader of the Conservative Party.

He held his first cabinet position in 1915, in the coalition government formed at the outbreak of The Great War. He was offered the top job by George V but stood aside in favour of the more experienced David Lloyd George. He served in Lloyd George's War Cabinet as Chancellor and was Leader of the Commons until 1922.

When the coalition collapsed, Chamberlain resigned as Party Leader, Lloyd George resigned as Prime Minister and Bonar Law stepped into both jobs. His main political concern when in power was the British war debt to America, and the much larger debts owed by Europe to Britain.

Chancellor Austen Chamberlain returned from negotiations with the Americans announcing he had promised that Britain would pay almost double what the Cabinet thought the country could afford. Bonar Law offered to resign but was persuaded to stay. He was subsequently diagnosed with throat cancer, which prevented speech. He resigned and died shortly afterwards, aged 65. There is a village called Bonarlaw, named after him, in Ontario.

A counter to Bonar Law is presented by British-born **Andrew Fisher**, who became Prime Minister of Australia three times: 1908-1909, 1910-1913 and 1914-1915.

Fisher was born in the mining village of Crosshouse in Scotland, was working in the pits by the age of 10 and a secretary of the local miners' union by 17. When his political activity made it impossible for him to find work at home, Fisher decided to emigrate to Queensland, Australia.

He ended up in the Gympie gold fields, where he taught himself philosophy and shorthand, joined the church, the defence force and the chess club, ran the Sunday school and bought shares in the local co-operative society. In his rise to power, Fisher spread his message by buying his own printing press and publishing *The Gympie Truth* to counter what he saw as a biased local press.

He was elected to parliament shortly before the Commonwealth of Australia was founded, lost his seat, regained it and was elected MP for Wide Bay in the first Federal Government, in 1901. He first became PM in 1908. However, his greatest mark was made in his second term (in the world's first Labour majority government), with the creation of the Australian capital state, Canberra.

Fisher brought in long-lasting restructured legislation aimed at redefining defence, the constitution, social security, finance, transport and communications. After resigning his third office as PM, Fisher became High Commissioner for Australia, based in London. He died in 1928 aged 66 and is buried in Hampstead Cemetery.

'Old Hickory', as **Andrew Jackson** was known when he entered the White House in 1829 aged 61, was the 7th President of America. Jackson spent much of his life fighting.

In his early teens, Jackson joined a rebel militia, was captured and permanently scarred by a British officer whose boots he had refused to polish. His ingrained hatred paid off when, in the 1815 Battle of New Orleans, Jackson's 5,000 soldiers won a victory over 7,500 British, killing or wounding more than 2,000 to Jackson's 13 killed and 58 wounded or missing. Jackson became a national hero, receiving a Thanks of Congress.

He was instrumental in displacing many indigenous tribes, and led troops in the Creek and Seminole wars in which thousands were slaughtered.

While military governor of Tennessee, Jackson was nominated for President in the 1922 and 1928 campaigns, the second of which he won. He unwisely invited his public to the White House after his inauguration, and the unruly crowd had to be lured back out again with alcohol. Jackson was reinstated in the 1932 election.

He was the first President to be targeted by would-be assassins. In 1835, mentally unstable house painter Richard Lawrence, who claimed to be Richard III, attempted to shoot Jackson. His pistols misfired, whereupon the President laid into him with his cane and had to be restrained by onlooker (and king of the wild frontier) David Crockett. Jackson died in 1845 aged 78.

The day after Abraham Lincoln was shot and killed at Ford's Theatre by John Wilkes Booth in 1865, Vice-president **Andrew Johnson** (1808-1875) became the 17th President of the United States.

Johnson had been fortunate; Booth's plan had been to have the three leaders of the Democratic government, including Johnson, assassinated in a single night. Johnson's appointed hitman lost his nerve.

Johnson was President during an era of great change in America, in the aftermath of the Civil War. He presided over the readmission of southern states into the Union, ejected the French from Mexico, bought Alaska (via Seward) from Russia, and survived two impeachment attempts by Congress. In retrospect, Johnson is considered to have been a poor politician, unable to take good advice and stubborn to the point of self-defeat.

Son of former Greek Prime Minister George Papandreou, **Andreas Papandreou** (1919-1996) was twice exiled from his country. The first time was when he was a student in 1936 and he was imprisoned and tortured by the Metaxas dictatorship and left the country to continue his studies at Harvard.

Decades later in 1967, after he had returned to Greece and become a politician, serving as chief economic advisor under his father's premiership, he was again arrested, this time by a military junta. His father died but Andreas fled the country, returning when the junta collapsed in 1974. He became Greece's first socialist Prime Minister in 1981.

He held power until political scandals forced his resignation in 1989. He was re-elected in 1993 but resigned three years later, shortly before his death.

Movers and shakers

Fiercely patriotic Scot **Andrew Fletcher** ((1653-1716) aka Andrew of Saltoun) was an inspirational orator and member of the Scottish parliament who argued through the latter part of the 17th century against the Act of Union between England and Scotland.

He joined forces against Charles II with the Monmouth rebellion (but shot and killed the Mayor of Taunton in a quarrel and had to flee abroad once more). He briefly joined forces with William of Orange but came to think him untrustworthy on the question of Scottish rule.

Fletcher became a formidable debater, issuing his 'twelve limitations' of the English parliamentary power over Scotland. Although these measures were not adopted, their essence survived in the 1704 Act of Security. Despite – and in part because of – his efforts, the Act of Union was passed in 1707. Fletcher bitterly retired from the fight and turned to agriculture.

Multi-lingual Norwegian-born **Andrew Furuseth** (1854-1938) was a sailor and labour leader whose work in building maritime unions and initiating legislation radically improved the lives of American seamen in the late 19th and early 20th centuries.

Furuseth was largely responsible for the Maguire Act (1895) and the White Act (1898), both of which reduced penalties for desertion in an age when the greatest threat of violence or injury came from one's fellow crew members. He was instrumental in creating the Sailors' Union of the Pacific (which he also led until the 1930s) and the International Seamen's Union.

Known eventually as 'The Old Viking', Furuseth was also the main architect of the 1915 Seaman's Act and the 1920 Jones Act, which took even greater strides to ensure mariners' rights. The Seaman's Act abolished imprisonment for deserters, cut punishments and regulated working hours, payment, food standards and safety. It also set minimum ratios for the number of qualified seamen aboard, and the number able to converse in the officers' language.

A monument to Furuseth stands in Romedal, the Norwegian village of his birth.

After his release from a Japanese PoW camp, **Andrew Gilchrist** (1910-1993) joined the Special Operations Executive (SOE), the wartime intelligence organisation formed by Churchill, as a spy working in India and Thailand.

After the war he moved from intelligence into diplomacy, becoming the British Ambassador to Iceland in 1956. He was in this post during the first Cod War – the British-Icelandic dispute over coastal fishing rights – and wrote about his experiences in *Rekyavik – Cod Wars and How to Lose Them*.

He was later posted to Chicago and then as ambassador to Jakarta – where the embassy was burned to the ground by supporters of the Sukarno regime. Gilchrist was knighted in 1964 before being sent as ambassador to Dublin – just in time for the posting of British troops to Northern Ireland in 1969.

He retired a year later for a quieter life as head of the Highlands and Islands Development Board. He died in 1993.

As the head and founder of independent think-tank Migration Watch, **Sir Andrew Green** (b.1941) is a controversial figure. Broadly respected as a highly experienced diplomat and an expert on the Arab world – he was British Ambassador to Saudi Arabia until his retirement in 2000 – Green's subsequent work on monitoring immigration has raised eyebrows. He has insisted, however, that Migration Watch is "neither hostile to immigration, nor racist".

Remember George W. Bush on September 11th 2001, sitting in a classroom as his chief of staff bent down to quietly inform him of the second plane to hit the World Trade Center?

The man with the news that appeared to paralyse the President in front of all those children was **Andrew Card Jr**.

The power of the chief of staff can be considerable. In some cases, the role has been seen as prime ministerial, acting just beneath, alongside or even in place of the US President. Card's run in the post was not, however, seen as especially influential.

He had serious rivals for the ear of the President from other, more confidential advisors. A former president of the now defunct American Automobile Manufacturers' Association and government liaison to General Motors, Card was also previously Secretary of Transportation to George H. W. Bush, who also assigned him to co-ordinate the relief effort following 1992's **Hurricane Andrew**.

Andrew Card formally resigned from office in 2006. Some say he was pushed.

Civil rights activist **Andrew Jackson Young Jr.** (b.1932) was a friend of Dr. Martin Luther King Jr., a former US congressman, a former mayor of Atlanta, Georgia, and America's first African-American ambassador to the UN.

He met Dr. King while campaigning to register African-American votes in the 1950s, and had become one of his main supporters and companions when King was assassinated in 1968.

He was a member of Congress for four years in the mid-1970s and was appointed as ambassador to the UN by President Carter in 1977. He was elected mayor of Atlanta in 1981 and was instrumental in securing the 1996 Olympics for the city. Since retiring from public life, Young's work for Nike with Good Works and with the Wal-Mart corporation have met with a mixed reaction to say the least. He no longer works for Wal-Mart, instead directing his energies into producing his own documentaries such as *Rwanda Rising*.

LORDS MAYOR OF LONDON

The Queens of England and Their Times by Francis Lancelott (1858) records that **Andrew Buckerel** (Lord Mayor 1231-1237), while visiting the royal buttery to serve King Henry III, mistakenly claimed "the honour of holding the King's wine-cup, and replenishing it whenever needed". Unfortunately, the King ordered that only "Master Michael Belot [the] Grand Butler of England, had a right to fill that office".

Accordingly, the chagrined mayor bowed to the royal will, and served the two bishops at the King's right hand.

Andrew Aubrey (Lord Mayor 1339-40 and 1351) was imprisoned, along with various other state officials including the Keeper of the Privy Seal, the Chief Justice, two bishops and – had he been available – the Archbishop of Canterbury, by Edward III.

The King had returned to England irritated that his latest taxes were not raising enough money to keep his many foreign creditors at bay. At that time the only English currency worth tendering abroad was wool, which was rather cumbersome.

Pupils and ex-pupils of Tonbridge School in Kent have former Lord Mayor of London (in 1550) **Sir Andrew Judde** to thank for their place of learning. A former skinner who rose to be a prominent merchant of the time, Judde founded the school in his home town in 1553.

According to *Wriothesley's Chronicle*, he "erected one notable free school at Tunbridge in Kent, and alms houses nigh St Helen's church in London, and left to the Skinners lands to the value of 60 pounds 3 shillings and 8 pence the year; for the which they be bound to pay 20 pounds to the schoolmaster, 8 pounds to the usher, yearly, for ever, and four shillings the week to the six alms people, and 25 shillings and 4 pence the year in coals for ever".

Sir Andrew Lusk (Lord Mayor 1873) was an alderman – a senior council judge – at the time of the Jack the Ripper murders in 1888.

An Andrew and a Scholar

Scottish theologian **Andrew Melville** (1545-1622) was a brilliant scholar who almost single-handedly resurrected teaching at Glasgow, Aberdeen and St. Andrews Universities in the late 16th century.

He spent his youth astonishing his lecturers at St. Andrews, France, Poitiers and Geneva and in 1574 returned to Scotland.

He taught theology, Hebrew, Chaldee, Syriac and the rabbinical languages. Melville and seven other clergymen of the Church of Scotland were summoned to London in order "that his majesty [James I] might treat with them of such things as would tend to settle the peace of the Church".

Melville wrote a sarcastic epigram about the rituals of Hampton Court which an eavesdropper repeated to the King. His reward was four years in the Tower. On his release, Melville was refused permission to return to Scotland, and ended his days as a professor at Sedan University in France. He died in 1622 aged 77.

<hr />

Record-breaking Andrews

Lancastrian **Andy Mapple OBE** is one of the world's most successful Elite slalom water skiers. He is an 11-times world record holder, 14-times US Masters Champion, 14-times US Open Champion, 14-times Moomba Masters

Champion, six-times World Champion and 12-times
Pro Tour Champion, with 169 professional victories
worldwide. Phew!

RAF Wing Commander **Andy Green OBE** (b. 1962) is the
current Land Speed Record holder and the first to break
the sound barrier on land. On 15th October, 1997, exactly
50 years and a day after the sound barrier was broken in
aerial flight by Chuck Yeager, he reached 763.035mph
(1227.99 km/h), the first supersonic record (Mach 1.016), in
ThrustSSC.

On August 23rd 2006, he set a new diesel world record in
the JCB Dieselmax of 350.092mph (563.418km/h).

In the Second Test against Australia at Edgbaston in August
2005, **Andrew Flintoff** broke Ian Botham's 1981 record
of six sixes in an Ashes Test Match with five in the first
innings, and a further four in the second innings. There's
more about 'Freddie' in the Sporty section.

British powerlifter **Andy Bolton** (b. 1970) was, in 2008,
the World Powerlifting Organisation three-lift world record
holder (1273 kg/2806 lb). Bolton also held the WPO world
records in the squat (550.5 kg/1213 lb) and deadlift (455
kg/1003 lb). He was the first to demonstrate a deadlift of
over 1,000 lb.

The aim of the Subway Challenge was to navigate the New York City Subway system in the shortest time possible. Bill Amarosa Jr., Michael Boyle, Brian Brockmeyer, Stefan Karpinski, Jason Laska and **Andrew Weir** set the Guinness World Record on December 28-29th 2006, with a time of 24 hours, 54 minutes and 3 seconds.

The fastest overland journey to the South Pole was completed by a team of five drivers including Britons **Andrew Regan** and **Andrew Moon**. The journey from Patriot Hills on the Antarctic coastline took 69 hours and 21 minutes.

A British golfing fourball of Ben Crosby, **Andrew Crawford**, John Lyon and Russell Hayhoe completed 18 holes in a record-breaking 1 hour, 4 minutes and 25 seconds at Ponteland Golf Course, Northumberland on June 19th 2005.

On January 9th 2006, **Andrew Lloyd Webber**'s *Phantom of the Opera* became the longest running musical on Broadway with 7,486 performances, beating the record held by his *Cats*. There's more about Webber in the Musical Andrews section.

The greatest number of different species spotted over 24 hours is 342, a record set by Kenyans **Andy Roberts**, Terry Stevenson and John Fanshawe at the 1986 Birdwatch Kenya event.

The longest solo flight ever in a hot air balloon is 16 hours and 34 minutes over 1066.2 miles, completed by American **Andy Clayton**.

Californian **Andy Macdonald** (b. 1973) is one of the world's best known skateboarders. He has his own range of ('Andy Mac') boards, shoes and helmets, has appeared in video games and even had a hand in designing an extreme pogo-stick called the Flybar 1200 (capable of jumping 7ft 6ins. in the hands of Guinness World Record holder Fred Grzybowski).

Macdonald is a 'vert' skateboarder (meaning he performs on ramps, as opposed to the street). He won the World Cup Skateboarding competition eight times.

American **Andy Linder** holds six world FootBag records, including for speed kicking (1,019 kicks in 5 minutes).

Canadian Paralympic gold medallist **Andrew Haley** holds six world records, four in butterfly events.

<hr>

YOUR ROYAL ANDREWNESS

Hungary has had three kings Andrew.

Andrew I (the White) returned to the throne from exile in about 1046 and reigned until unseated by his brother in 1060.

A century and a half later, **Andrew II** − who had fought long, hard and unsuccessfully to take the throne from his brother King Emeric − inherited the throne when first Emeric, and then the king's infant son died.

Andrew III was Andrew II's grandson. He took the throne in 1290 after the assassination of King Ladislaus, but several others − a man pretending to be Prince Andrew of Slavonia, Ladislaus's wife, her son and her grandson − announced claims.

Estate agent **Prince Andrew Piikoi Kawānanakoa** (b. 1964), Prince of the House of Kawānanakoa, is the third in line to the Hawaiian throne. Prince Andrew also owns and manages Keauhou Kona Farms. His English name comes from his grandfather, Andrew Anderson Lambert. Andrew's eldest son, Prince Andrew Kaeokulani Kawānanakoa, is fourth in line to the Hawaiian throne.

Prince Andrew of Greece and Denmark, (b. 1882), was married to Princess Alice, the great granddaughter of Queen Victoria. Alice's relations put her in a distant line to the British throne, while Andrew's even more extenuated line came from his mother, who was descended from George II's eldest daughter.

He commanded the Second Army Corps in the Greco-Turkish War but was court-martialled for disobedience in 1922 and banished from Greece. He took up exile in Britain and published a defence of his actions. He was eventually given back his title and land. The prince visited briefly but ended his days on a yacht in the south of France.

Andrew Albert Christian Edward Windsor, otherwise known as **Prince Andrew, Duke of York** (b. 1960), is currently fourth in line to the British throne. He was second until the births of Charles's sons, William and Harry. Andrew served in the Falklands War in the Royal Navy aboard the HMS Invincible. He flew both offensive and rescue missions as a Sea King helicopter co-pilot throughout the campaign.

He retired from active service in 2001, and was made an Honorary Captain in 2005. Prince Andrew's relationship (marriage and divorce) with Sarah Ferguson is unusual in having remained friendly and co-operative. They live in nearby properties – he at Royal Lodge in Great Windsor Park, she in Dolphin House in Surrey – and have shared custody of their two daughters.

They even co-habited for a short while in early 2008 after a fire at Dolphin House made it temporarily uninhabitable, and have holidayed together as a family. Andrew is not without critics, being nicknamed 'Airmiles Andy' from his love of frequent flying. He once hired a private jet with £100,000 of taxpayers' money for a tour of the USA, and on another occasion used the Queen's Flight to attend a golf tournament.

SAINTS

There is more than one **Saint Andrew**. Here are the best known…

Saint Andrew the Apostle (b. early 1st century AD) was the younger brother of Saint Peter and a son of Jonah, or John. He was born in Bethsaida, on the Sea of Galilee, where he and Peter were fishermen. Andrew was a disciple of John the Baptist, whose testimony first led him and John the Evangelist to follow Jesus. He at once recognised Jesus as the Messiah, and hastened to introduce him to his brother.

Andrew is said to have been martyred by crucifixion, on an X-shaped cross (he considered himself unworthy of Christ's form of crucifix) at Patras in Achaea. His feast day is November 30th.

Saint Andrew is the Patron Saint of Scotland, Russia, Greece and Romania. His Scottish feast day is 30th November. The flag of Scotland is the **Cross of St. Andrew**. The Order of Saint Andrew, or the Most Ancient Order of the Thistle, was established by James VII of Scotland in 1687; it is a knighthood restricted to the king or queen and sixteen others.

Saint Andrew the Scot (Scot here meaning 'Gael' rather than Scottish person) was born in the 9th century in Ireland. He studied under Saint Donatus of Fiesole, whom he accompanied on a pilgrimage to the holy places of Italy.

Saint Andrew of Crete was an 8th century Damascan bishop, theologian and hymnographer (someone who writes, or writes about, hymns). Andrew was mute until the age of seven, when it is said he was miraculously cured after receiving Holy Communion. He is also known as Andrew of Jerusalem.

Andrew of Constantinople is among the 10th century saints who pretended to be Fools for Christ, and is also known as Andrew the Fool or Andrew Fool-for-Christ-sake.

Born Slavic, Andrew was said to have had a vision of Most Holy Theotokos in the Vlahern Church of Constantinople.

Saint Andrew Kim Tae-gon was Korea's first Roman Catholic priest, in the early 17th century. His father was martyred for practicing Christianity, which was prohibited in Confucian Korea.

Many thousands of Christians were executed during the Joseon Dynasty. In 1846, at the age of 25, Andrew was tortured and beheaded.

Andrew Dũng Lạc was a Roman Catholic saint and martyr, executed by beheading in 1839. His feast day is 24th November.

Saint Andrew Bobola was a Jesuit missionary and martyr. In 1657 he was captured in Lithuania by the Cossacks of Chmielnicki and subjected to torture. His limbs were amputated, his skin flayed, he was burned, wood spikes were driven beneath his fingernails and his nose was cut off. He was killed.

Saint Andrew Avellino was a 16th century Italian saint. He changed his name from Lancelotto to Andrew on entering the order of the Theatines.

SCIENTIFIC ANDREWS

Mathematicians

In 1995, British mathematician **Professor Sir Andrew Wiles**, a professor at Princeton University specialising in number theory, published a proof of Fermat's last theorem.

The theorem had been puzzling mathematicians since the 1800s and all attempts at a general proof had failed. Building on the work of many famous mathematicians, Wiles finally proved it using a method that could not have been known to Fermat.

The actual proof is very indirect, and involves two branches of mathematics which at face value appear to be unrelated. Now you know!

Soviet mathematician **Andrey Kolmogorov** advanced various scientific fields including probability theory, topology, logic, turbulence, classical mechanics and computational complexity.

In 1925 Kolmogorov graduated from Moscow State University to study under Nikolai Luzin, whom he later subjected (with Pavel Alexandrov) to political persecution in what became known as the 1936 Luzin affair. In 1933, Kolmogorov published *Foundations of the Theory of Probability*, establishing himself as the then leading expert in the field.

Andrey Markov was a Russian mathematician best known for his work on the theory of stochastic processes. His research later became known as Markov chains. In 1913 the council of Saint Petersburg elected nine scientists honorary members of the university.

Markov was among them, though his election was confirmed only after the revolution in 1917. He lectured in probability theory and calculus of differences until his death in 1922.

MEDICINAL ANDREWS

Sir Andrew Fielding Huxley, an English physiologist and biophysicist, is included in the Nobel & IgNobel section.

Sometimes referred to as the founder of modern human anatomy, **Andreas Vesalius** was an anatomist and physician. He was the author of the hugely influential *De humani corporis fabrica* (1543), which discussed various bodily systems including the circulatory system, muscles, bones, nerves and internal organs, and included comparatively accurate drawings by Titian pupil Jan van Calcarson.

While a professor at the University of Padua, he performed public dissections of cadavers. He made enemies by denouncing his illustrious forebears Aristotle and Galen, well ahead of his time, and suffered restrictions to his work and public vilification as a result.

Natural history

The true contribution of Scottish naturalist **Andrew Graham** (b. 1815) to natural history was discovered only recently. A study of the Hudson Bay Company's archives revealed that the credit for many of the observations and countless specimens he sent to London throughout his career in Canada in the late 18th century had been plagiarised by others.

Mineralogy & Geology

Seven-times Mayor of Penzance and mineral collector **Andrew Ketcham Barnett** was Principal of the Penzance School of Mines (now part of the Camborne School of Mines).

He lectured on mining, helping to build their mineral collection, and was an original member of the Mineralogical Society, a Fellow of the Geological Society from 1875, and President of the Royal Geological Society of Cornwall 1907-1908.

Andrew Lawson was the US-based geologist who first identified and named the San Andreas fault, after the 1906 earthquake. He was born in 1861 in Anstruther, Scotland.

Geography

One of the world's most widely read geographers is **Andrew Goudie** (b. 1945). The Master of St. Cross College, Oxford, he specialises in desert geomorphology and climate change in the tropics, and has written best-selling books on the human impact on the environment.

Physics

No relation to Andrew Fielding Huxley, **Andrew D. Huxley** (b. 1966) is the chair of the physics department at Edinburgh University. He has performed breakthrough research into superconductivity evoked by extremes of pressure or temperature.

Chemistry

Spanish-Mexican scientist **Andrés Manuel del Río Fernández** (1764-1849) discovered the chemical element vanadium in 1801, though it took half a century for other scientists to verify his claim by isolating it for the first time.

He named it eritronium. Nils Sefstrom, who rediscovered it, gave it the name vanadium after Vanadis, the Scandinavian goddess of love.

German chemist **Andreas Libavius** wrote the first systematic chemistry textbook, *Alchemia*, in 1597.

Electricity

French physicist **André-Marie Ampère** (1775-1836) was one of the main discoverers of electromagnetism or, as he called it, electrodynamics. The SI unit of measurement of electric current, the ampere, is named in his honour.

PUGH

SPORTING ANDREWS

<u>Cricket</u>

It's almost fair to include **Andrew 'Freddie' Flintoff** (b. 1977) alongside George Best and Paul Gascoigne in a list of sportsmen for whom it was just a bit too easy to be brilliant. But although he shares their penchant for self-destruction, there remains a realistic hope that Flintoff's best is yet to come.

The disproportionate number of replaced roof tiles and windows around Lancashire's St Anne's ground bear testament to Flintoff's hitting power at the age of 12. In one junior match he hit so many sixes that the match had to halt while both teams searched for balls. His career is a list of dazzling performances interspersed with terrible form, poor fitness, injuries and binge drinking.

The 2007 Cricket World Cup was a low point. Only months after having captained England to a 5-0 defeat in the 2006-7 Ashes, he began the tournament – a match against New Zealand – with a golden duck (bowled by the first ball of the match).

That night he was rescued at sea after drunkenly falling off a pedalo, and was stripped of his vice-captaincy. In 2009, Flintoff held the record for the most sixes, with 68 scored for England since his 1998 debut.

Six-foot-six fast-medium bowler **Andy Caddick** (b. 1968) is a domestic, and former England, player. Born in

Christchurch, New Zealand, Caddick toured England before settling in the country and playing his whole career to date at Somerset County Cricket Club, where he is vice-captain. He has taken more than 200 Test wickets for England and was one of the five Wisden Cricketers of the Year in 2000.

South African all-rounder **Andrew Hall** was a member of the national team from 1999 to 2007. He made his Test debut in 2002 against Australia and took a maiden 5 wicket haul (5 for 18) against England in the 2007 Cricket World Cup.

In 2003 he enjoyed a stint with Worcestershire and in 2005 was an overseas player at Kent. Hall made the headlines in 1998 when he was reportedly mugged and shot in the hand at a cashpoint machine.

Known as 'Smudge', **Andrew 'Mike' Smith** was a swing bowler for Gloucestershire, and played a single Test for England at Headingley in 1997 against Australia. He became a solicitor on his retirement from the sport.

British-born Australian cricketer **Andrew Symonds** (b. 1975) is a right-handed batsman who was selected for an England tour of Pakistan but pulled out in order to win a place in the Australian side.

His occasionally glittering career was sullied when he was at the centre of the 'monkey' racism row with an Indian cricketer in 2007-8. Symonds was subjected to racist chants by the Indian crowd during the One Day Series in India, and a row erupted in 2008 at Sydney Cricket Ground when Symonds claimed he had been called a 'monkey' by spin bowler Harbhajan Singh.

Singh received a three-match ban, but this was lessened to a fine after further investigation revealed he had probably, as he claimed, been swearing in Punjabi. If so, he had called Symonds something far worse than a monkey, but without the racial overtones. Since this incident, and the backlash over Aussie 'sledging' in Test matches, Symonds appears to have lost interest in the game. He was dropped from the 2008 One Day side.

<u>Football</u>

The world's first black international footballer (for Scotland, 1881-2), and the first to play in the FA Cup (for London Swifts, 1882), was **Andrew Watson**. He was born in Demerara, in what was then British Guyana, in 1857. Watson played mostly in Scotland as a left- or right-back and in the years he played enjoyed two emphatic victories over England: 6-1 in 1881, 5-1 in 1882.

Brother Walfrid (1840-1915) – known before his conversion to the Irish Marish Brotherhood as **Andrew Kerins** – founded The Celtic Football Club in 1887. Born to crofter parents in County Sligo, north-west Ireland, Walfrid moved to Scotland in the 1870s where he became a teacher and headmaster. His aim for the football club was to raise money for the poor of East Glasgow.

Five years after setting up Celtic, Walfrid was sent to London's East End where he organised children's football tournaments in Bethnal Green and Bow. He was described by former Celtic player Tom Maley as "a wonderful, organising power... of lovable nature" and a man who "only had to knock, and it was opened".

Nottingham-born **Andrew Cole** (b. 1971) – better known as Andy, though he has since requested the use of his full name – is among the highest scoring players in English football history. With 187 Premier League goals, Cole is the second highest scorer behind Alan Shearer.

He has 15 caps for England, and in club football played for Arsenal, Fulham (on loan), Bristol City, Newcastle United, Manchester United (where he was a record goal scorer, once netting five goals in one match against Ipswich), Blackburn Rovers, Fulham again, Manchester City, Portsmouth, Birmingham City, Sunderland, Burnley and home-town club Nottingham Forest.

In a 1999 low point, Cole released the rap single Outstanding. In the video, he name-checks himself frequently while cruising a neighbourhood in his Aston Martin. It reached number 69 in the UK charts.

Andy Herzog (b.1968) is Austria's most capped player of all time, with 103 caps and 26 goals. He played in the 1990 and 1998 World Cups.

Andy Johnson is a striker. As at January 2009, he plies his trade for Premier League outfit Fulham. His previous clubs include Birmingham City and Crystal Palace.

A poster of Johnson indicating "3-0" in the 2006 game against Liverpool was sent to every Everton season-ticket holder. Johnson earned a couple of caps in 2005 and has played in World Cup qualifiers.

Welsh international **Andy Johnson**, on the other hand, plays for Barnsley, having represented Norwich City, West Bromwich Albion, Leicester City and Nottingham Forest.

Andy Robinson is a Leeds United player, who has previously played for Cammel Laird, Tranmere Rovers and Swansea City.

Former Manchester City, Everton and Sheffield United player **Andy Hinchcliffe** (b. 1969) was capped seven times for England. In 1993, Finnish composer Osmo Tapio Raihala wrote an orchestral work inspired by him. He's now a radio commentator.

Andy Sinton (b. 1966), a QPR midfielder, was capped a dozen times for England without scoring.

A hat-trick of Andy Grays

Former Crystal Palace midfielder **Andy Gray** (b. 1964) is
a one-cap wonder who played for his country in 1991 in a
Euro '92 qualifier. He's now Head Coach for Sierra Leone.

Andy Gray (b. 1977) is a Yorkshire-born Charlton Athletic
forward with caps for Scotland.

Former football hero and now pundit **Andrew Mullen
Gray** (b. 1955) had a glittering career in the 1970s and '80s
– winning England's golden boot (for scoring the most goals
of the season) in 1976/77, scoring the winning goal for
Wolverhampton Wanderers in the 1980 League Cup final,
and one of the winning goals in the 1984 FA Cup final for
Everton.

He was capped 20 times for Scotland, scoring seven goals.
These days, though, he's best known for his commentary
on Sky Sports – with catchphrases "Top drawer", "Take a
bow, son", "Easy height for the keeper" and many others.
The tabloids have nicknamed him Randy Andy after recent
'love rat' behaviour. He has five children by four different
women.

Andy Beattie (1913-1983) played seven matches for
Scotland in the late 1930s, and in 1954 became the national
squad's first manager. The Swiss-hosted 1954 World Cup
was not a happy event, though. Only four games with a

squad of 13 players left him feeling handicapped, and he resigned. The team was knocked out after losing 7–0 to Uruguay.

The longest throw-in in football, at up to 41m, used to belong to Welsh international **Andy Legg** (b. 1966), who was last seen playing for Llanelli. He has six caps for Wales.

Tennis

British tennis player, Glaswegian **Andy Murray**, is (at the time of writing) ranked the fourth-best tennis player in the world. His brother, Jamie, is the UK's highest ranking doubles player.

Murray was at Dunblane Primary School in 1996, aged 9, at the time of the Dunblane massacre.

He first came to public attention in 2005 when he reached the third round of Wimbledon. In 2006, Murray won his first ATP title, the SAP Open in San Jose, California, by beating Andy Roddick and Lleyton Hewitt.

At Wimbledon, he reached the fourth round of a Grand Slam for the first time, after defeating third seed Roddick. Murray was one of only two players – the other being Rafael Nadal – to beat Roger Federer in 2006. He has gradually climbed the rankings since then. At Wimbledon in 2008, in his first career Grand Slam quarter-final, Murray was defeated by eventual champion Rafael Nadal.

The Scot suffered a surprise defeat at the 2008 Summer Olympics in the first round but reached the final of the US Open, losing in straight sets to Roger Federer. Murray has recently described himself as "Scottish, but also British".

Former number one **Andy Roddick** (b. 1982) is, at the time of writing, ranked 7th in world tennis. Roddick first became a Grand Slam singles champion at the 2003 US Open.

He reached three other Grand Slam finals but lost to Roger Federer each time.

Roddick holds the record for the fastest serve in professional tennis (155mph). In 2005, he won the Arthur Ashe Humanitarian Award of the Year for of his charity efforts, and in 2007 the Andy Roddick Foundation was awarded by the Arthur Ashe Institute for Urban Health.

Rugby

Clive Woodward's 2003 Rugby World Cup-winning reign was a hard act to follow and the job of head England coach fell to former Bath and England flanker **Andy Robinson,** OBE, in October 2004.

After a less than glittering run, he resigned in November 2006. He now coaches Edinburgh and Scotland A XV.

Who is the greatest ever Scotland full-back? It could be former Scottish international **Andy Irvine**. He won 51 caps as full-back for Scotland between 1972 and 1982 and also earned British Lions caps. He was considered an inspiring player whose mere presence distracted rival team members, and whose running from the back could be both incisive and decisive. He is an inductee of the Scottish Sports Hall of Fame and the International Rugby Hall of Fame. Irvine became president of the Scottish Rugby Union in 2005.

Others might say Irvine's successor in the No. 8 shirt, **Andrew Hastings** – known by his middle name of Gavin – better deserves the top spot in the full-back hall of fame. Gavin Hastings, OBE, won 61 caps for Scotland (20 as captain), and led the British Lions in the 1993 New Zealand tour. His point-scoring record speaks for itself.

He was, for a long time, the all-time record scorer in the Scottish national rugby union team, with 667 points in Test matches. He remains the all-time record points scorer for the British and Irish Lions (in Test matches) with 66 points. He scored 17 tries for Scotland, to place him third on Scotland's all-time list.

Perhaps the tallest prop in international rugby, 6ft 5ins. power-lifter **Andrew Sheridan** has made his mark on the sport in recent years, partly through his enormous strength.

He won his first cap for England in November 2004 and was selected for the 2005 Lions tour of New Zealand. He made his presence felt that year in the Test against Australia by grinding the Australian front row into submission. Both opposition props retired before the end of play. Sheridan won Man of the Match against Australia in the 2007 Rugby World Cup.

Theology student **Andrew Trimble** (b. 1984) plays at outside centre or on the wing for Ulster and Ireland. He made his debut for Ireland against Australia during the 2005 International Rugby Board Autumn Internationals.

Trimble made the 22-man squad for Ireland's 2006 Six Nations Championship match against Italy, and also featured as a second-half replacement against France where he scored a try. Trimble's 6 tries in 16 games for Ulster and performances in the autumn internationals and Six Nations, earned him the BT Irish Rugby Union Players Association's Newcomer of the Year award.

Running

Design and Technology teacher and British international road and fell runner **Andi Jones** (b. 1978) came fourth in the 2003 WMRA (World Mountain Running Association) World Mountain Trophy in Alaska.

He runs for the Salford Harriers at home, where he won the 2006 and 2007 North of England Cross Country Championships and the 2006 Liverpool Half Marathon.

Andrew Carter (b. 1949) represented Great Britain at the 1972 Munich Olympics, qualifying for the men's 800m final. This was a legendary race.

American Dave Wottle seemed to have been outclassed, running 20 metres behind the field. USSR's Yevgeny Arzhanov took the lead in the final corner, steaming past Kenyan front-runners Robert Ouko and Mike Boit. Arzhanov thought he had won, but Wottle shocked everyone with a surprise sprint and took gold by a fraction of a second. Carter came sixth, with no medal, but had a great view of a memorable final.

British triathlete **Andrew Johns** competed at the first Olympic triathlon at the 2000 Sydney Olympics and came 16th at the 2004 Athens Olympics.

Boxing

Polish-born Andrzej Golota – referred to as **Andrew Golota** (b. 1968) since his move to the US – is a heavyweight boxer who struggled to live up to his apparent potential. Twice in 1996 he lost to former champion Riddick Bowe when ahead on points after being disqualified for low blows.

In 1997 he had a shot at title holder Lennox Lewis but was KO'd in the first round. In 2000 he faced Mike Tyson but walked out of the ring after being felled in the first round. He fought twice for the world title in 2004, but lost to Chris Byrd in April and John Ruiz in November. In 2005 he fought WBO world champion Lamon Brewster but was knocked down three times in the first round in a fight that lasted less than a minute.

Guyanan light-middleweight **Andrew 'Six Heads' Lewis** beat James Page in 2001 to win the vacant WBA Welterweight title. He lost the title in a rematch (after a previous bout was stopped because of Lewis's cuts) to Ricardo Mayorga in 2002. In 2007 Lewis's uncle, Abdel Nur, gave himself up as a suspect in the JFK International Airport terror plot.

Swimming

Andy Jameson's voice will be familiar to anyone who watches the BBC swimming coverage, where he's a regular race commentator. He competed in the 1980 Moscow, 1984 Los Angeles and 1988 Seoul Olympics, taking bronze in the 100m butterfly at the latter.

He retired from competitive swimming in 1989. His sister Helen was also a swimmer, and represented Britain at the 1980 Olympic Games in Moscow, winning silver in the 4 x 100m medley relay.

Andrew Astbury competed for Great Britain in the 1980 Moscow and 1984 Los Angeles Olympics, winning bronze in the 4 x 200m freestyle relay at the latter. At the 1982 Commonwealth Games in Brisbane, he won the 200m and 400m freestyle races in Commonwealth record times.

Andrew Clayton competed at the 1996 Atlanta and 2000 Sydney Olympics for Great Britain. He won the 1997 European title in the men's 4 x 200m freestyle relay.

Andrew Hunter came sixth in the Beijing 2008 men's freestyle relay final.

<u>Wrestling</u>

Not to be confused with gigantism, acromegaly is a growth-hormone disorder that causes overall physical enlargement, in particular the hands, feet and facial features.

Among famous sufferers are Richard Keil, who played Jaws in two James Bond movies, and both of the actors who played Lurch in *The Addams Family*: Ted Cassidy in the TV series and Carel Struycken in the movies.

At least five famous professional wrestlers were also acomegalic: Giant Silva, The Swedish Angel, The Big Show, The French Angel and **Andre The Giant**. A French actor and wrestler standing (officially) 7ft 4ins. tall, Andre Roussimoff ascended to the peak of the World Wrestling Federation championship in the 1970s and 1980s.

In the latter part of his career, by which time he had turned from 'babyface' to 'heel' (the two pro wrestling character types), Andre held an ongoing and very lucrative feud with Hulk Hogan. Wrestling was big in those days.

The pair's 1987 fight at Wrestlemania III still holds the highest recorded attendance figures – more than 93,000 – of any US indoor sporting event. Andre played Fezzik, a role he greatly enjoyed, in *Princess Bride*, and Big Foot in a two-part episode of *The Six Million Dollar Man*.

Andre died in 1993. He had refused treatment for his condition, and although he'd outlived his prognosis by six years, he died at 46.

Motorsport

Andy Priaulx, MBE (b. 1973), is the only FIA Touring Car champion to win an international-level championship for four consecutive years (2004-2007). He is the 2008 European Touring Car champion, and a three-times World Touring Car champion.

Aussie **Andrew Jones** is a V8 Supercar driver for his uncle's team, Brad Jones Racing. He won the 2004 Konica Minolta series – the second tier of Australian V8 Supercar racing – but has had less success since his move up to the lead series.

Motorcycle speedway rider **Andy Smith** won the British Speedway Championship in 1993, 1994 and 1995, one of only three riders ever to achieve this feat.

Golf

Australian **Andrew Buckle** won the 2002 Queensland Open on his professional debut. In 2006 he finished second in the Indonesia Open and the TCL Classic. He won a PGA Tour card at the 2006 Qualifying School.

Scottish golfer **Andrew Coltart** has two wins on the main European Tour, the 1998 Qatar Masters and the 2001 Great North Open. In 1995 he was a member of the winning Scottish team in the Alfred Dunhill Cup, and won the Australian PGA Championship in 1994 and 1997. He was a member of the European Ryder Cup team in 1999.

American **Andrew Magee** (b. 1962) is the only golfer in PGA Tour history to hit a hole-in-one on a par-4 hole – at the 2001 Phoenix Open on the 17th hole.

British golfer **Andrew Murray** played on the European Tour from the late 1970s to the mid 1990s, winning the 1989 Panasonic Open.

Bolton-born **Andrew Oldcorn** recovered from ME before winning the 1993 Turespana Masters Open de Andalucia, the 1995 DHL Jersey Open and the 2001 Volvo PGA Championship.

Scotsman **Andrew Strath**, born in 1836, began his working life as an apprentice club maker. He won The Open Championship in 1865, and finished in the top four in 1860, 1863, 1864 and 1867. He died of tuberculosis aged just 32.

US golfer **Andy Bean** (b. 1953) has 11 PGA tour victories to his name, though he never won a major championship. He was a force to be reckoned with on the PGA Tour from 1977 to 1986. He now plays on the Champions Tour, and won the 2006 Greater Hickory Classic at Rock Barn and the 2008 Regions Charity Classic.

Badminton

Britain's number one player and Olympic participant, **Andrew Smith**, was born in Portsmouth in 1984.

Darts

Known when playing as 'Pieman', Bromsgrove-born darts professional **Andrew Smith** (b. 1967) has won three PDC (Professional Darts Corporation) Pro Tour titles, and in 2007 won the PDPA (Professional Darts Players Association) Scottish Players Championship.

Traditionally, the Pieman fares better in 'floor' events – untelevised tournaments featuring many boards playing simultaneously.

Skateboarding

Professional Florida skateboarder **Andrew Reynolds** (b. 1978), also known as Drew, The Boss, Spock or Turtle Boy, is the founder and owner of Baker Skateboards.

Football and cricket Andrews

Rangers' 'Greatest Ever Goalkeeper' (according to a 2001 fans' poll) **Andrew Goram** (b. 1964) was born in Lancashire but played both football and cricket for Scotland. He won 43 caps in the No. 12 goalie shirt, and played four cricket matches for the Scottish team.

Brixton-born **Andrew Ducat** (1886-1942) was one of the few men to have represented his country in more than one sport. He played football for England six times, scoring his only goal against Wales in 1910.

Ten years later he was named a Wisden Cricketer of the Year. He scored 52 centuries for Surrey but, because of frequent injuries, played only one Test match. In one county game he was 'out' twice in one innings, when the ball smashed his bat: the ball was caught and a splinter dislodged the bails. He is also the only cricketer in history to have died while playing at Lord's cricket ground. He had a heart attack during a wartime Home Guard match.

ANDREWS IN STRANGE DEATHS AND SUICIDES

An argument over chocolate cake icing between a New Jersey father and his 10-year-old son ended in the death of the former, who was called **Andrew** (and is a Darwin Award winner).

In the midst of a heated argument, Andrew challenged his son to plunge a five-inch kitchen knife into him if he hated him so much, and offered the blade. After at first refusing, the boy acquiesced, killing his father. His last words were: "Would you believe the kid did that?"

Andy Lewis, the original bassist of Australian band The Whitlams, committed suicide in February 2000, aged 33.

Australian adventurer **Andrew McAuley** (b. 1968) was presumed to have died following his disappearance at sea while attempting to kayak 1600km across the Tasman Sea – between Australia and New Zealand – in February 2007.

Andreas Baader (1943-1977) – of the Baader-Meinhof Gang (aka Red Army Faction) – committed suicide in his cell after being convicted of several murders and other crimes.

He entered a suicide pact with fellow members on learning that the Red Army Faction's attempt to hijack a plane to secure their release had failed. Before his death, Jean-Paul Sartre visited him in his cell, and later referred to him as "incredibly stupid" and "an arsehole".

Known to many at the University of California, Berkeley, in the early 1990s as The Naked Guy, **Andrew Martinez** (1972-2006) was an American football player and activist who, from 1992, insisted on appearing naked at all times.

He fought and won many battles for his right to do so – it was legal for a time to go about nude in Berkeley – as there was nothing lewd or aggressive in his behaviour.

He appeared on countless daytime chat shows, but was eventually expelled from university and began travelling throughout Europe, where his mental health declined.

Martinez was arrested and charged with battery and assault in 2006. He suffocated himself with a plastic bag in his cell at Santa Clara County Jail, San Jose, California. He was 33.

⟫●⟪

TV & RADIO ANDREWS

Andrew Davies' name – these days appearing above rather than below the title of TV plays and series – has become something of a seal of quality. He wrote the campus-based medical comedy drama series *A Very Peculiar Practice* and many of the best historical adaptations seen on British TV in the past two decades.

Pride and Prejudice, Vanity Fair, Sense and Sensibility and *Middlemarch* are all Davies' work. To that impressive list you can add *House of Cards* and *To Play the King*, not to mention *Bridget Jones's Diary* (he collaborated on both Helen Fielding movies).

His other specialisation is children's TV, in which field he created *Marmalade Atkins, Conrad's War* and *Alfonzo Bonzo*. Newer Davies projects include the adaptation of *Brideshead Revisited* for the cinema and *The Book Group*, based on the TV series by Annie Griffin.

The most popular radio show in Australian broadcasting history is **Hamish & Andy**, featuring comic DJs Hamish Blake and Andy Lee. The show is broadcast to about two million daily listeners in the afternoon drive-time slot. The pair favour quirky, people-centred ideas that actively involve the listeners.

Their competition to invent a new potato crisp – The People's Chip – was very popular and culminated in the manufacture of a limited run of free gravy-flavoured crisps.

The People's Greyhound, on the other hand, was a racing dog called Fred Basset, bought and raced by the pair. Hamish and Andy also travelled to Afghanistan – by popular demand – to broadcast their show for the Aussie coalition troops.

Andy Rooney (b. 1919) is a veteran US comedy radio and television writer, famous for *A Few Minutes With Andy Rooney* on *60 Minutes*.

An unequalled champion of music from all corners of the world, Lancastrian **Andy Kershaw** (b. 1959) is a highly respected broadcaster and journalist who once worked as a roadie for Billy Bragg. He spent 15 years fronting a world music evening programme on Radio 1 before relocating to Radio 3 in 2000.

He was awarded honorary doctorates by the universities of East Anglia (in 2003) and Leeds (2005). Sadly, he has been absent from the airwaves since 2007.

Following the break-up of his marriage that year, he was jailed three times for breaching a restraining order placed on him with regard to his former partner and their children.

As this is written, he is in hiding from a year's jail sentence, for breaching the restraining order again, on the Isle of Man.

Andy Kane, better known as **Handy Andy** from *Changing Rooms*, has also appeared in the US version of the programme, *Trading Spaces*.

He also appeared on the LIVINGtv reality show *I'm Famous and Frightened!* and the Sky One show *Cirque de Celebrité*.

This was followed by *Increase Your House Price By Ten Grand*, another makeover programme, and a series of BBC Primary Geography programmes.

Handy Andy is also a US brand of children's carpentry tools, a 1934 film starring Will Rogers and a strip in the comic *Krazy*.

A veteran of *Byker Grove*, in which he played Ben Carter, **Andrew Hayden-Smith** is now best known as a face of CBBC and the *UK Top 40 Show*.

Andrew Günsberg, popularly known as **Andrew G.**, is the co-host of the reality series *Australian Idol*. He was born in England in 1974, became an Australian citizen in 2000, and was named Cleo magazine's 'Bachelor of the Year' in 2004.

Andrew Collins is a prolific British journalist, author, DJ and broadcaster on popular culture. He co-writes *Not Going Out* with Lee Mack, is a former scriptwriter for *EastEnders*, *Family Affairs* and the sitcom *Grass*, and is film editor for *The Radio Times*. He's one of a growing collection of pundits who are called upon to reminisce between clips about any TV subject of which the nation might have 100 favourites.

He wrote an autobiography of Billy Bragg (*Still Suitable for Miners*, last updated 2007) and an entertaining three-part memoir: *Where Did It All Go Right* (2003); *Heaven Knows I'm Miserable Now* (2004); and *That's Me in the Corner* (2007). He and Richard Herring now produce a fortnightly podcast called *Collings and Herrin*.

In an interview with Radio 6, Collins revealed that the first record he bought was Blockbuster by The Sweet, and that he wished he'd written the lyrics to Tank Park Salute by Billy Bragg.

"Then I'd know what the title meant (he won't tell anyone)."

TV presenter and executive **Andi Peters** (b. 1970) began as the unfortunate human sidekick of Edd the Duck in

The Broom Cupboard on Children's BBC in the early 1990s, followed by *Live & Kicking* for three years. He was executive producer of *Top of the Pops* and created the T4 strand on Channel 4.

He competed in ITV's *Dancing on Ice*, co-hosted *Sunday Feast* and *The All Star Talent Show*. He owns a modelling agency and was runner-up in the third series of *Celebrity MasterChef* in July 2008.

Amos 'n' Andy was a US radio sitcom that ran, in varying formats, from 1928 until the end of the CBS repeats in 1966. It was one of the world's first radio comedies.

———◆———

WEALTHY ANDREWS

Forbes magazine drew up a list of the 200 wealthiest historical figures by calculating their net worth at their peak, adjusted to current values. Highest on the 2008 list was John D. Rockefeller; second was **Andrew Carnegie** with $298.3bn.

Carnegie emigrated to Pennsylvania, USA, from his native Dunfermline as a child in 1848. As a boy he worked in a cotton factory with his father, but the first part of Carnegie's adult career concerned the accumulation of capital.

A bright, charming and conscientious worker, he rose through the ranks of the Pennsylvania Railroad Company in the run-up to the Civil War. His clever maximisation of profits and shortening of journey times made him enough money to begin a series of profitable investments.

In the second phase of his career, Carnegie acquired controlling interests in the coke, iron and steel industries. He devised a method for mass-producing rail lines at a time of explosive growth, and bought steelworks, coalworks, iron fields, railways and steamships before amalgamating his holdings into the Carnegie Steel Company in 1892.

By 1901 he was ready to retire. Carnegie then began the third and most famous era of his life, that of a philanthropist. Importantly, he did not give to charity but we could fill this book with the list of institutions, including 2,500 libraries, that bear his name.

On his death in 1919 aged 83, Carnegie had donated more than $350m. He once wrote:

"There is no class so pitiably wretched as that which possesses money and nothing else."

The same chart that puts Carnegie second in the world has **Andrew Mellon** (1855-1937) sixth. Mellon, as his name happens to suggest, was extremely well rounded. An extremely successful entrepreneur and investor in his early life, Mellon was one of a handful of Americans whose bank balances grew to extraordinary sizes on the back of the Industrial Revolution.

Mellon concentrated his finances on founding and backing such eventual giants as ALCOA, Carborundum, Koppers, and Gulf Oil. His fortune amassing nicely, in 1921 he stepped on to the political stage at the invitation of President Warren Harding. As Secretary of the Treasury, with America still deep in debt from the war effort, he drastically cut income tax on the wealthy in an effort to get more people to pay it. It seemed to be working but the Great Crash of 1929 sent the country into freefall.

Mellon was disliked by Hoover and resigned in 1932 to become – briefly – British Ambassador. On his return to the States a year later, he began amassing important artworks until he had the largest collection in the country, including six works Stalin's men quietly removed from the Hermitage in St. Petersburg to raise money for the Kremlin. He died while fighting tax evasion charges but was eventually cleared.

The fate of the Kissel brothers is among the oddest in recent American history. Robert Kissel, 40, was killed by his wife in what became known as the 'milkshake murder'. Nancy Kissel, who was having an affair, drugged her husband with a milkshake and then bludgeoned him to death with a lead statuette.

She slept with his body for two days in their multi-million dollar Hong Kong apartment before rolling him up in a rug and ordering workmen to collect and dispose of it. Three years later in 1996, the body of Robert's brother **Andrew Kissel**, 46, was found bound and stabbed in the basement of his Greenwich, Connecticut house.

Real estate developer Kissel was fighting his wife for custody of his brother's children and reportedly on the point of admitting guilt in a multi-million dollar fraud case.

Although he had amassed substantial assets, a conviction would have put him in jail for some years. It is still not known who killed Andrew Kissel, but two years after his death in March 2006 his chauffeur and another man were charged with his murder. One theory police had not dismissed was that he paid them to kill him so that his children would benefit from what would have been his one remaining asset – a life insurance policy.

Andrew Michael (b. 1980) sold his web-hosting business – Fasthosts – in the nick of time. In the next year, 2007, hundreds of websites were shut down when customers' personal details were hacked and stolen. Michael spends at least some of his £46 million stake hiring or persuading B-list celebrities to attend parties and functions.

On one occasion he arranged for The Darkness to play at his local football ground, hosted by Jonathan Ross. He also once invited a group of disadvantaged children to his home, and surprised them by unveiling the Sugababes, Girls Aloud, Rachel Stevens and Big Brovaz as the evening's entertainment. He's at number five on *The Times' Young Rich List*, and equal 746 overall.

Also officially young and wealthy are **Andrew Gower,** who runs and owns £104m of a computer game business Jagex, and tennis star **Andy Murray**. Discover more about the Scottish athlete in the Sporting Andrews section.

WHAT DOES ANDREW MEAN, EXACTLY?
A type of authentic ghetto moustache.

USAGE:
*"That's a nice **Andrew** you've got going on there, need to thin it out a bit though... can't see your lips!"*

<hr>

WHAT DOES ANDREW MEAN, EXACTLY?
To suddenly cancel a very important event without direct communication. Cancellation is usually performed via emails, text messages or other impersonal means.

USAGE:
Chap one: "Oh my God, Tom and I were so supposed to hook up on Friday..."
Chap two: "Awesome!"
*Chap one: "Yeah, until he **Andrewed** me"*
Chap two: "How did he do it?"
Chap one: "Email..." (rolls eyes)

There is every chance we have missed an Andrew, or two.

Let us know at **www.stripepublishing.co.uk**

ACKNOWLEDGEMENTS

First, I'd like to thank my publisher Dan Tester for the original opportunity, and his help and encouragement.

To complete a book like this, on such a narrow (and yet also surprisingly broad) subject, it helps to have some personal interest.

For that reason it is my parents I must thank for deciding to call me Andrew – shortly after christening me Philip.

It's good to be an Andrew.

Lord knows how I could have continued into the small hours in search of the wider world of Philip. Thanks also to my partner Natalie Wilkie, my neighbour Maryclare Foa, and Zooey and Dalfy for their tea and encouragement.

BIBLIOGRAPHY

Andy Goldsworthy (1990), *Stone* (1994), *Wood* (1996), Andy
Goldsworthy Viking

If I Should Die: A Death Row Correspondence, Jane Officer, New
Clarion Press 1997

The Locomotive Builders of Kilmarnock, Russel Wear, Industrial
Railway Society, 1977

The Magician's Nephew, C. S. Lewis (1955)

The life and work of A. A. Markov, Gely P. Basharina, Amy N.
Langville, and Valeriy A. Naumov (Elsevier 2004)

Lives of the Saints, Alban Butler (Continuum 1985)

Recommended websites

The Internet Movie Database – www.imdb.com
The Guardian Group – www.guardian.co.uk, www.
filmreference.com
The Biography Channel – thebiographychannel.co.uk
The Internet Broadway Database – www.ibdb.com

www.andrethegiant.com
www.iucnredlist.org
www.amonline.net.au
www.cms.int
www.boglewood.com/palladio
www.eng.archinform.net
www.britannica.com
www.andrewdasburg.com
www.andrewlogan.com
www.alternativemissworld.co.uk
www.andrewrogers.org
www.andrew-vicari.com
www.warholfoundation.org
www.edu.warhol.org
www.news.bbc.co.uk
www.s9.com
www.jsc.nasa.gov
www.obspm.fr
www.mporzio.astro.it
www.taschen.com
www.adsabs.harvard.edu
www.news.com.au
www.cnn.com
www.cfo.com

www.willamette.edu
www.cases.justia.com
www.tarlton.law.utexas.edu
www.tupolev.ru/english
www.intel.com/pressroom
www.everestnews2004.com
www.comedycv.co.uk
www.ipl.org
www.electricscotland.com
www.About.com
www.eetimes.com
www.geo.ed.ac.uk
www.ipl.orgwww.sfmuseum.net
www.brompton.co.uk
www.DirectorsNews.co.uk
www.Bnet.co.uk
www.GlobalSecurity.org
www.mybrestfriend.com
www.inventblog.com
www.Journalisted.com
www.andregide.org
www.bartelby.com
www.crumey.toucansurf.com
www.kcl.ac.uk
www.agreeley.com
www.andrewharvey.net
www.andrewjefford.com
www.newcriterion.com
www.jimstringernovels.com
www.gutenberg.org
www.contemporarywriters.com
www.andrew-roberts.net

www.andrew-taylor.co.uk
www.vachss.com
www.ukraine-observer.com
www.andymcnab.co.uk
www.andy-nicholls.co.uk
www.middlemiss.org
www.historyofwar.org/articles/people_cunningham.html
www.spartacus.schoolnet.co.uk
www.junobeach.org/e/3/can-pep-can-mcnaughton-e.htm
www.summitpost.org
www.andrewbird.net
www.sirandrewdavis.com
www.andrewkeeling.ukf.net
www.sara.uea.ac.uk
www.thevorticist.co.uk
www.jacksmannequin.blogs.com
www.dailymail.co.uk – 'Loser who had the last laugh'
www.russocentral.com
www.wolfmother.com
www.vonoeyen.com
www.andrewwk.com
www.wammybox.com
www.creation-records.com/ride/andy.html
www.andybell.com
www.erasureinfo.com
www.andygibb.50megs.com
www.andyirvine.com
www.andylaverne.com
www.thesweet.com
www.andywhite.com
www.nobelprize.org
www.en.beijing2008.cn

www.avo.alaska.edu
www.Geonames.org
www.albertafirst.com
www.number10.gov.uk
www.ljsvendsen.com
www.whitehouse.gov
www.tudorplace.com.ar
www.georgiaencyclopedia.org
www.migrationwatchuk.com
www.sportfocus.com
www.news.bbc.co.uk
www.thrustssc.com
www.andrew-bolton.com
www.freddieflintoff.com
www.cricinfo.com
www.royal.gov.uk
www.freepages.genealogy.rootsweb.ancestry.com
www.4dw.net
www.newadvent.org
www.stx.ox.ac.uk
www.eps.berkeley.edu
www.kolmogorov.com
www.mathforum.org/dr.math
www.lms.ac.uk
www.bronwenwilson.ca
www.olympics.org.uk
www.pgatour.com
www.andycaddick.com
www.cricketarchive.com
www.footballdatabase.com
www.Icons.com
www.andrewjones.com.au

www.boxrec.com
emericaskate.com
www.100greatblackbritons.com
www.furd.org
www.sporting-heroes.net
www.soccerbase.com
www.andymurray.com
www.andypriaulx.com
www.andyroddick.com
www.atptennis.com
www.irishinbritain.com
www.england-afc.co.uk
www.listafterlist.com
www.rfu.com
www.xroads.virginia.edu
www.officialandipeters.com
wherediditallgoright.com
www.handyandydiy.com
www.cbsnews.com
www.fox.com.au
www.pbs.org
whokilledandrewkissel.com
www.trutv.com
www.nydailynews.com